Deep Sea Treasure

Deep Sea Treasure

Mark Williams

Heinemann : London

William Heinemann Ltd
10 Upper Grosvenor Street, London W1X 9PA

LONDON MELBOURNE TORONTO
JOHANNESBURG AUCKLAND

First published 1981

© Mark Williams 1981

SBN 434 86660 1

Printed and bound in Great Britain by
Morrison & Gibb Ltd, London and Edinburgh

*THIS BOOK IS dedicated to all divers—
professional and amateur, but in particular to those few,
leaders and divers, who by their skill, tenacity and
scholarship have reaped rewards of treasure, both
intrinsic and historic, and by their success inspired
hundreds, perhaps thousands of divers throughout the
world, awakening a compelling interest in the history
and treasure beneath the sea.
Therefore, to the memory of the late Kip Wagner; to
Roland Morris, Robert Sténuit, Rex Cowan and Robert
Marx in acknowledgment of the debt we owe them for
their example—for showing the way.*

Contents

Illustrations

Author's Acknowledgments

I am most grateful for the considerable help received from many sources —especially from Roland Morris, Rex Cowan, Robert Sténuit, the Trustees of the late Kip Wagner, L. Flanagan of the Ulster Museum, David Burrell, E. J. de Vries of the Maritiem Museum Prins Hendrik, Rotterdam, the Burton family of Teignmouth.

In England
The British Records Office. The British Museum. The National Maritime Museum, Greenwich. Rochester Public Library. Kent County Archives. Devon Association Papers. Torquay Public Library. City of Exeter Public Library. *The Western Morning News. The Daily Telegraph.* David & Charles Publishers, Newton Abbot. Sotheby Parke Bernet & Co., London. W. H. Lane & Sons, Penzance. Bernard Eaton. Frank Gibson, St Mary's; Max Wright, St Agnes, Isles of Scilly.

In Holland
The Netherlands Maritime Institution, Rotterdam. The Maritiem Museum Prins Hendrik, Rotterdam. The Scheepvaartmuseum, The Hague. Sotheby Mak van Waay, Amsterdam. The Koloniaal Archief, The Hague. The Historisch Museum, Amsterdam. VOC Archive papers in Rotterdam, Middelburg, and Dordrecht.

From Spain
Papers of The Office of the Indies, Seville.

From the U.S.A.—Florida
Papers of the Florida State Museum, Department of Marine Archaeology. University of Florida papers.

Isles of Scilly

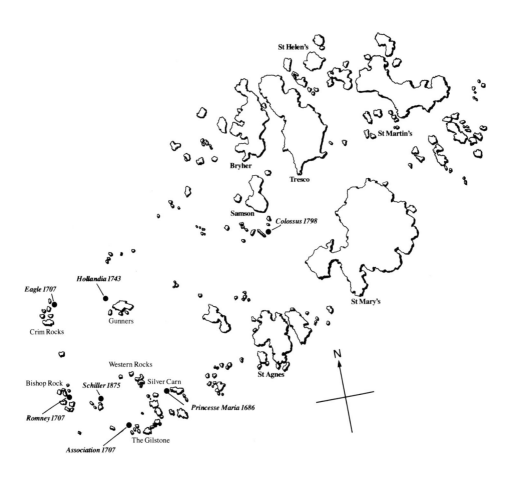

St Helen's

St Martin's

Bryher

Tresco

Samson

Colossus 1798

Hollandia 1743

Eagle 1707

Crim Rocks

Gunners

St Mary's

Western Rocks

Bishop Rock

Schiller 1875

Silver Carn

St Agnes

N

Romney 1707

Princesse Maria 1686

Association 1707

The Gilstone

Map of Scillies showing principal wrecks.

Introduction

Stories of lost treasure are very old indeed and treasure hunters have been trying to sort out the reality from the myth for almost as long. There are still enormous 'troves' lying hidden or lost in various corners of the world. One of the richest and least explored corners is at the bottom of the sea, where treasure ships have been piling up for centuries.

It is only recently that it has become possible to recover some of this treasure. The last decade, in particular, has seen an upsurge of activity by divers working with equipment that has at last given them some freedom of manoeuvre in deeper waters. But even today treasure hunting on the sea bed is a hazardous operation, among shifting sands and boulders and in dangerous channels.

The lure is enormous, of course, and the promise of riches irresistible. But the objects themselves have a fascination quite as great as their worth. A gold ring, exquisitely fashioned some four hundred years ago, inscribed with a lover's phrase—'No tengo mas que darte' (I have nothing more to give thee)—speaks with a rare pathos even to the toughened adventurers we shall be meeting in our story. Golden chalices, pieces-of-eight, beautifully wrought jewellery, cunningly carved cannon—slowly but surely the under-water treasure seekers of today are building up a vivid picture of ages long gone by.

I

Deep Sea Treasure

Here are great galleons, once the pride of mighty navies, fleets carrying gold and silver from the New World to the Old, merchant vessels bearing luxuries from the East. The treasure hunter must trace the story of his prey carefully to the moment of disaster, searching old documents for clues about its cargo, its crew, its destination and the circumstances of its sinking. Like a jig-saw puzzle, the pieces of information fit together in an intriguing mosaic to enable the treasure hunter to identify the scattered remains of a particular ship, centuries old, resting somewhere under the mud beneath millions of square miles of ocean.

It is an exciting story. The oceans and the treasures they conceal are, in a way, the last true adventure frontier. The men who dive in search of their secrets are among the last great explorers.

What *is* the lure that has turned them into treasure hunters?

We could do worse than start with Doug Rowe. . . .

I

The Prize beneath the Waves

'The sea is a more hostile environment than space.'
Astronaut Scott Carpenter

In a cloud of white dust, Doug Rowe liberally sprinkled himself with baby's talcum powder from a giant-sized economy tin. Grunting with the effort, he pulled on his black neoprene skin suit. A companion hoisted a pack of air cylinders, taking the weight as Rowe clipped the harness on. Next a sheathed knife was fastened to his shin and then followed a lead weightbelt and swimming fins for his feet. Rowe was almost ready to dive again.

He dipped a hand into the sea and rubbed the cooling water over his face, sweating now in the hot sun. He spat into his face-mask, smearing the saliva over the glass before washing it clear again and slipping it over his head. Rowe positioned the mouthpiece of his demand valve so that it felt comfortable and took a couple of experimental breaths. He pulled down his face-mask; his blue eyes sparkled from behind the glass, his curly blond beard surrounded the rubber frame and droplets of seawater rolled down to cluster in beads, catching the sun, looking for all the world like rows of glistening pearls amongst the fair hair.

Rowe sat on the gunwale, facing inboard. He gestured with one hand to the others and then, judging the surging Atlantic swell, rolled backwards into the sea from the pitching launch.

3

Immediately his surface world of blue sky, fleecy white clouds, wheeling seagulls and warmth was exchanged for a bitterly cold, green world full of turbulence. Minute air bubbles momentarily clung in their thousands to his black wetsuit, breaking off to join those racing to the surface from his air cylinder pack.

The sounds of the surface—burbling diesel engines, waves slapping against hull, voices in conversation—all ceased. His new world was quiet but not wholly silent. His ears attuned to modulated sounds: the threshing of great fronds of brown kelp weed waving to and fro in pulsing currents, flowing first one way and then reversing and pulling weed and small boulders along in their wake; odd squeaks as weed slid against weed; a hollow knocking from stones swirling up and settling again to the sea bed in time and motion to the stream. Heavier clumps of sound came as great fissures of granite separated and then were forced together by the pressure of the sea, grunting and grating with the tremendous force, puffing out particles of rock in a fine dust cloud. And all the time there was the reassuring sound of the air valve opening and closing.

Jagged outcrops of rock about him and below warned of dangers for the unwary. Caverns and ravines beckoned. Canyons of dark shadows held chilling invitations to explore, yet briefly halted even the experienced diver with a shiver of fear for the unknown. All around him, Doug Rowe could see every shade of green and brown and black. As he finned deeper, his clear vision gave way to a hazy indistinct fog. Swirling particles of broken weed, sand and debris hung suspended, moving, twisting, tumbling to endless whirls and eddies. For a moment he paused, allowing his body to adjust to the cold, glancing up a second to the surface, now some forty feet above, moving and heaving like a giant mass of mercury shot with shafts of light green sunbeams.

Most people think of the coastal sea bed in Europe as a flat plain covered in dull brown sand or ooze, silent and bare. It is simply not true. As on land, there are green meadows, but of weed. There are hills and mountains, valleys and ravines and caves, rock, mud—a land submerged. The topography is similar below to the immediate land mass above. If there are granite outcroppings above, they are almost certain to occur below. Even the weather is reflected. A raging gale produces a twisting, surging current.

All is certainly not silent and tranquil beneath the seas, particularly in the Western Approaches of the Atlantic Ocean, where the Scilly Isles are exposed to huge Atlantic swells that travel thousands of miles to crash and vibrate with frightening power upon the first obstructions in their path, flinging masses of white water angrily into the air.

No intentional wrecker of ships could plan a better trap than the one nature has drawn with the coastline of the Scillies and England's West Country. Like a giant leg thrust out into the Atlantic, Cornwall's granite cliffs stride across two busy shipping lanes—the English Channel and St George's Channel. As if that were not enough, the hundred-odd islands and rocks that make up the Scillies archipelago stretch a further forty-three miles out into the ocean, a trap for unwary shipping.

It is little wonder that diving in the Scillies is a seasonal activity that avoids winter storms when eighteen-foot tide races roll giant boulders of fifty tons or so along the sea bed. Even in summer, each tide can alter a section of sea bed explored and charted just the day before. Hundreds of shipwrecks are known to be in that region but few have been found. The shifting sea bed grinds and pounds most things in its path, timbers of sailing ships, spars and masts, keel frame and cargo. No wreck would retain the recognizable form of its hull for long. A rounded ballast stone or a corroded cannon would be the best clue one might hope for in the search for one of the lost wooden sailing ships of the past with which our story is concerned. It is barely conceivable that anything of value could remain for hundred of years on such a sea bed. But there were those who believed such a possibility existed.

Doug Rowe was one of the believers, a wiry Cornish diver, well experienced in West Country waters. He continued his surveying, constantly checking the whereabouts of his companion diver. No one with any sense dives alone. Rowe and his mate belonged to a team of divers hired to explore this particular site on the Western Rocks for clues to a centuries' old shipwreck. On this summer's day in 1967, he finned still deeper, down into a ravine between underwater granite cliffs.

He soared and wheeled with the sea bed in arm's reach. Around and about, above and below a jumbled mass of granite boulders and kelp weed, his black-suited frame trailed its silver bubbles behind.

5

The barque Cromdale *stranded near The Lizard in dense fog in 1913. It was hoped to salvage her—if the weather remained calm. But the Western Approaches are seldom calm for long.* (F. E. Gibson)

Suddenly, among all the greens and browns, glinted a hint of yellow. Quickly Rowe extended a hand and picked up what was obviously a gold coin, lying free on the sea bed between two rocks. He held it close to his face-mask. The coin appeared to be in mint condition. It felt comfortably chunky, without a trace of surface tarnish, as though it had been lost only that day, yet the coin bore the date 1706 and had been in the sea for 260 years.

It is difficult to express elation at a depth of fifty feet. You cannot yell with delight—a mouthpiece prevents such excitement. Doug Rowe turned a complete somersault in a welter of bubbles and headed for the surface, glancing around for his mate, gesturing the universal signal for 'top-sides'. He burst through the skin of the sea into bright sunshine and spat out his mouthpiece. With a great whooping cry, he attracted the attention of those on the launch and, within seconds, the coin was being closely examined, glinting in the sun with a dull rich hue. It was the first gold coin ever retrieved from a sunken English man o'war in home waters.

A gale blew up ripping off sails. Heavy seas pounded the once elegant Australian wool clipper into matchwood. One more casualty among hundreds in the Approaches to the English Channel. (F. E. Gibson)

The 1706 4,000 reis piece brought to the surface by Doug Rowe from the Association *in almost perfect condition despite its 260-year sojourn in the sea.* (Benbow/Morris Collection)

The coin bore on the obverse a Cross of Jerusalem with the date 1706 and the Latin inscription -IN-HOC-SIGNO-VINCES-; on the reverse, an Imperial Crown surmounted a shield and the inscription -PETRVS-II-D-G-PORT-ET-ALG-REX- (Peter II, King of Portugal and Algarva)—alongside the shield was the number 4,000. This meant that the coin was a 4,000 Reis piece minted in Brazil, an incredible find worth hundreds of pounds. Far more important was that it provided a clue to what else lay fifty feet beneath their feet. The strong possibility existed that the *Association*, a great English man o'war, wrecked in 1707, a treasure ship of enormous value—an Admiral's flagship, no less—lay within reach. Subsequent research would show that the Spanish port of Vigo would play a part in the wreck's identification. Led by Roland Morris, the diving team became increasingly optimistic about further exploration. They were on the verge of great discoveries.

There is nothing new about coincidences. In the same year, 1967, almost to the day of Rowe's discovery, 250 miles north at Lacada Point near the Giant's Causeway in Northern Ireland, Robert Sténuit, a Belgian diver, made an equally astonishing find. Forty feet down, below soaring black cliffs to the north of Dunluce Castle, Sténuit was on the trail of a Spanish wreck from the Armada of 1588. This was a Neapolitan galleass, the *Girona*, and the Spanish port of Vigo played its part in the story of this wreck too. Sténuit had been diving the waters of Europe for twelve years, looking for sunken gold. He had found bronze cannon and many artifacts of historical importance during those years but never, until this moment, a piece of gold.

Lacada Point was an appalling place to dive, open to the Atlantic rollers with black rocks and needle-sharp reefs. Boulders and stones moved in time with the currents. Three days previously, Sténuit had spotted a cannon but then had an agonizing wait for the weather to improve so that he and his companion, Marc Jasinski, could mark the spot. When at last the weather became a little kinder, they moored their rubber dinghy and dived once more into the icy sea. The cannon had been lying clear three days previously, now it was covered by rocks and boulders. While Jasinski photographed the cannon, Sténuit spotted a flat, round, grey pebble. It was no ordinary pebble: a faint Jerusalem Cross was just discernible—a silver piece-of-eight. And then they found another lying on the sea bed at the entrance to a cave.

Sténuit dived again, digging around with an iron bar, shifting boulders. Then he found an iron cannon ball heavily encrusted with a concretion of iron oxide and sea growth known as 'crud'. As he dug deeper, he came on other cannon balls and another piece-of-eight, this one well preserved with the arms of Spain clearly etched and showing a capital 'T' with a small 'o' beneath, T̥, denoting the Toldeo Mint. Then, miraculously shining, Sténuit spotted a gold object between two stones, not a coin but a tiny ring. It was his first gold from the sea depths. Now he was sure that he had the evidence to show that he had found a Spanish Armada wreck. And so it proved. Robert Sténuit had found the wreck site of the *Girona* and in his hand he held a gold ring that had survived an incredible 379 years on the sea bed.

Sténuit realized the importance of his find. There would be much to do, much to organize but first to inspect the ring. The thin gold band had an opening and, exquisitely made, a tiny hand held out a heart; inscribed around the band, 'No tengo mas que darte'—'I have nothing more to give thee'. It was a sweetheart's ring, after the fashion of the day, a sad artifact, for the lady who gave the ring would never have seen her lover again. In its own way, the ring graphically demonstrated the tragic toll of human life in every shipwreck. The modern diver is constantly surrounded by evidence of such tragedy.

Deep Sea Treasure

Roland Morris and Robert Sténuit are two of the most energetic and professional treasure hunters at work today. For nearly forty years Roland Morris had dreamed of discovering and diving on the wreck of the *Association*, (1707) flagship of Sir Cloudesley Shovell. For much of that time, Morris, a craggy Cornishman, had donned a copper diver's helmet and clumped his way around West Country waters in lead-soled boots, cutting up steel wrecks. With his own small firm based in Penzance, he earned his living as a salvage diver. But above all, Morris was an historian with a passionate interest in ships and crews of the seventeenth and eighteenth centuries. Morris is unique in Marine Archaeology in the United Kingdom, although he is too often underestimated for his historic and nautical knowledge. He is the doyen of British treasure seekers.

His knotted forearms and battered hands testify to a hard working life but he is still wiry and tough, although now in his late sixties. His voice is soft and gentle to the ear; a faint, attractive West Country burr falls pleasantly in conversation and those strong hands, used to working with all kinds of wood, can hold a thin pencil and fashion detailed and accurate scale drawings of old sailing ships. When the opportunity at last arose for Roland Morris to realize his dreams, he was too old to dive himself. He was to see and experience much of the excitement through younger eyes, the eyes of a team of divers he himself trained. The outcome was well worth the considerable heartaches and the difficulties of raising money in the early days.

Roland Morris walks with the rolling gait of a seaman, habitually wearing a faded blue denim cap perched rakishly above humorous brown eyes; a greying beard epitomises the seafarer, an oldtime smuggler, a buccaneer of the past perhaps. There can be nothing better for those who are interested than to sit in a corner of his 'Admiral Benbow' restaurant in Penzance, a drink in one hand, to listen to the tales of shipwreck around the Cornish and Scilly coasts. Ideally, it should be in winter with a howling gale outside and rain lashing the empty streets and Morris's quiet voice demanding a compelling interest: 'It was in the 'thirties—the *Bessemer City* struck just to the west of St Ives and broke in two. Difficult it was— nothing but rocks below and the steep cliffs; we rigged a "blondin" and got to her by overhead line. She wouldn't last but a few days.'

He pauses, takes a sip of his 'shrub' and begins again: 'General cargo she carried. Motor cycles, timber, zinc and thousands of tons of tinned food'. His eyes twinkle, 'Folks had a good old "rummage", I can tell you. There was a lot of tinned salmon on the table in West Cornwall for a few days. . . .'

Wherever seamen, fishermen and divers gather, tales are told. These are always absorbing but, in the more remote areas of any coast, such tales, rich in folklore, take on added authenticity. For years Morris listened to tales of oldtime wrecks, the wrecks of sailing ships of long ago and he would often be shown a relic or artifact to support a particular tale. These tales, together with his avid reading, gradually enabled Morris to assimilate a vast knowledge of the subject.

A giant bower anchor from Association *lying on St Mary's Quay, Isles of Scilly, after recovery by the Morris team. The anchor is eighteen feet in length with a breadth of twelve feet, a typical stocked anchor used by the Royal Navy throughout the eighteenth and nineteenth centuries.* (F. E. Gibson)

Deep Sea Treasure

Robert Sténuit, the Belgian diver, was once a student of politics at Brussels University. He became fascinated by the fictional underwater world of American writer Art Rieseberg and gave up his studies to become a professional diver. He set a Belgian record for depth of dive and his diving expertise led to a friendship with Henri Delauze, President of COMEX of Marseilles, a company that manufactures diving systems and all the types of technology for underwater engineering that modern industry—oil exploration and the like—require. With the financial assistance of Henri Delauze, Sténuit's life took on a regular pattern. During the winter he researched in museums and libraries throughout Europe. In the summer he led diving expeditions to locate likely sources of oldtime wrecks, diving on the remains of English, French, Dutch, Russian and Spanish men o'war and East and West Indiamen. It was in Vigo he first heard of the *Girona*, a 1588 Armada galleass. Over the years he built up a bulky file on the Spanish treasure ship.

Sténuit is a rare animal in marine archaeology—administrator, organizer, team leader, diver, researcher and writer, he does it all and very successfully too. Now in his late thirties he keeps himself very fit. Tall, slimly built, he nonetheless has the physical strength needed to battle with underwater elements. His diving teams, mostly French, enjoy a loyalty and camaraderie hard to equal. Sténuit has a wonderful sense of humour matched by his diving and photographer colleague, Marc Jasinski. Together these two have roamed most of the world's seas and experienced the high and low points of treasure seeking.

On the face of it, Roland Morris and Robert Sténuit are poles apart—in age and background—yet they share a remarkable affinity. They love the detective work of research, painstakingly poring over old documents, accumulating the knowledge so vital to their work. Their interest had been aroused enormously by discoveries made in 1955 by a prematurely white-haired American, then in his forties, who stumbled on a vast treasure.

It was in Florida that the late Kip Wagner set off a wave of interest in underwater treasure that rippled its way across the Atlantic and crashed upon the shores of Cornwall and Belgium. Wagner found the wrecks of a Spanish treasure fleet. By location and upbringing, he was as far removed from the sea, ships and their history as it was possible to be. His business was the construction industry and he lived in Ohio, a long way from the Atlantic Ocean, even farther from the Pacific or the Gulf of Mexico. In the late 1940s he moved to Florida to build an hotel near the small town of Wabasso where an area of almost virgin, desolate coastline lay close, some forty miles south of Cape Kennedy. Called Sebastian Inlet, it is a narrow pass littered with rocks and sand bars. At high tide it is just navigable but full of racing cross-currents. Low tide reveals a frightening coral and rock strewn sea bed.

From Sebastian south to Wabasso, a long stretch of beach, over a hundred yards wide at low tide, meanders between reef-pocked and steep sand dunes, scrub-covered in places. It is the sort of beach successive storms alter, carving new inlets, covering whole areas with new sand, ripping sand from others, revealing deeply buried rocks.

Wagner took to exploring the beaches. Many times he heard tales by Wabasso oldtimers of coins picked up along the sands. Not really believing their stories, nonetheless he kept his eyes open on his strolls but in those early days never saw a thing. And then, one day, walking on the beach with a fellow worker, Wagner was surprised when his companion picked up seven silver coins in less than half an hour. Eagerly Wagner examined them and realized why he had never picked any up before. The coins were black, irregularly shaped and of various sizes. Oxidized black by electrochemical action, they looked more like pieces of flint rock than silver.

Wagner consulted his local library and checked out the coins, learning they were 'cobs', as the old colonists called them—'Cuba de Barre' in Spanish. These were cut from a bar of silver, fashioned by hand until the silver reached a weight equivalent in value to eight Reales, then hand-pressed and stamped with the arms of Spain on the obverse and the Cross of Jerusalem on the reverse—the original of the fabled pieces-of-eight. For the purists, it was the coin with the machine-milled edge of circa 1750 that was the true piece-of-eight.

With these coins, Wagner began the work of research, that might give a clue to the ship that had once held the silver. This research led Wagner to the reported loss of a Spanish treasure fleet in 1715, wrecked by a hurricane and sunk near Cape Canaveral (as it then was—Cape Kennedy today).

He formed a company—the Real Eight Company—and the

serious work began, work that extended over many years and produced staggering results. Even in the first years, Kip Wagner's name was soon splashed around the world, with finds of hundreds of pieces-of-eight, gold rings and ingots of pure gold—one weighing more than seven pounds. In time Wagner and his company brought specie and plate to the surface worth millions of dollars. Wagner's finds confirmed that even after hundred of years on the sea bed, coin, gold and silver of colossal value could be retrieved.

By the middle 1960s a number of like-minded divers and researchers were actively at work. The sand on the sea bed was explored in summer; in winter, the exploration continued in the archives of museums. In England, a London solicitor, Rex Cowan, assisted by his wife, began to concentrate on the old files of the Dutch East-India Company in Holland.

During the Second World War, Rex Cowan had been evacuated to the United States to complete his education, returning to England and the Royal Air Force for his National Service. Later, a Law degree at London University was followed by a solicitor's practice in North London. Cowan has the tough look of a boxer about him, although he is not a diver himself. It is amazing how many of that fraternity have features resembling pugilists of many rounds' standing. Cowan is a fine team leader, a good administrator, meticulous about his records and his research. Qualities that led him to underwater success.

So, following Kip Wagner, came a new generation of treasure seekers to the West and East of the Atlantic Ocean. In Europe, there were Roland Morris, Robert Sténuit, Rex Cowan, Sydney Wignall, Alan Bax, Colin Martin, Richard Larn and others; in the United States, there were Wagner, Robert Marx, Teddy Tucker, James H. Keegan and Paul Tzimoulis among the many. Professional and amateur, young and not-so-young, their dreams were very similar. They knew the treasure was on the sea bed and they knew now that some, at least, could be retrieved. But part of the essential research was to find out how it got there in the first place.

2

The Great Treasure Fleets

No tale of sunken treasure can be told without a background word about the search for new territories over which to claim sovereignty, about merchant princes, their ships, captains, routes, the cargoes and, of course, how the treasure came to be on the sea bed.

It was the inability to sustain an overland route from Europe to the East that led to the exploration of the possibility of an ocean highway. Henry, Prince of Portugal (1394–1460), provided money for voyages of exploration to Asian and African coasts, earning by his patronage the title of 'the Navigator'. From Portuguese and Spanish purses came gold to finance ships and expeditions, although such purses did not always open willingly and often provided financing too thin for the good of ships or men.

Many of the more successful expeditions are well known. In 1488, Bartholomew Diaz rounded the Cape of Good Hope. Vasco da Gama discovered and named Natal, crossed the Indian Ocean to Calicut, and thus became the first European to round the Cape and reach India by sea. Columbus (Christobel Colon, to give his true name) sailed west from Seville, endeavouring to find a western route to India and China and discovered instead the West Indies, South America and parts of Central and North America. How fitting that his sarcophagus, a magnificent monument supported by four Indian statues some ten feet high, stands in Seville Cathedral.

Magellan discovered the strait which was named after him and sailed the Pacific islands through to the Philippines. One of his ships completed the first circumnavigation of the world. Another fine Portuguese navigator was Pedro Alvares Cabral, who discovered Brazil. From France, Cartier, Ribault and La Salle explored with equal prowess.

It was Pope Alexander VI who, gazing at a rough map of the time, imperiously drew a vertical line down the Atlantic and declared all new land discoveries would henceforth either belong to Spain or Portugal—west of the line to Spain, east to Portugal.

The Spanish and Portuguese colonial aspirations were further galvanized into action. In 1508 the Portuguese discovered Sumatra; in 1510 Goa became their main base in India. Malacca was captured in 1511, Moluccas in 1513. Portugal dominated the Spice Islands for the next seventy years and established numerous trading bases throughout India.

Unfortunately for the Iberian partners, Alexander's Papal Decree fell on very stony ground in England and Holland. The 'Heretic Pirates' went their own way, raiding ships and settlements at will.

England engaged in sea exploration on a much smaller scale. Henry VII sent John Cabot to find a northern sea route to Cathay; instead Cabot discovered and explored parts of North America. John's son, Sebastian, undertook later voyages in search of a north-west passage to China, roaming around what would become known as Hudson's Bay. Dutch navigators and explorers also left their mark and names throughout this great century of discovery— The Barents Sea, Spitsbergen, Staten and Rhode Island, Manhattan, the Tasman Sea, Van Diemen's Land, New Zealand.

New territories were discovered and charted, claimed on behalf of the sovereignty of the explorer's sponsor and later exploited for the exotic and unique merchandise these lands could provide for a greedy Europe. By far the greatest number of territorial claims were made by Spain and Portugal; by the time of Philip II's assumption of the Portuguese throne in 1580, Spain ruled four of the world's six continents and every sea save those of Northern Europe and the African Mediterranean Coast.

Philip II's titles spanned the world: King of Aragon, Castile, Leon, King of Sardinia and the Two Sicilies, King of Navarre, of Granada, Toledo, Valencia, Galicia, Mallorca, Seville, Cordoba,

Corcyra, Marcia, Jaen, the Algarve, Algeciras, Gibraltar, the Canary Islands; Ruler of the Guinea, Angola, Mozambique, the East Indies, the West Indies, the Spanish Main; King of Portugal, of Algarva, Brazil, the Azores, the Cape Verde Islands; Ruler of the India Settlements; Governor of Aden, Muscat, Ormuz, Java, the Moluccas, the Philippines, Macao; Archduke of Austria; Duke of Milan, of Limburg, Brabant, Luxembourg, Guelders; Marquis of Antwerp; Count of Hapsburg, Burgundy, Tyrol, Barcelona, Flanders, Artois, Hainault, Namur, Holland, Zeeland and Zutphen; Lord of Biscay, Molina, Overijssel, Tournai, Groningen, Utrecht and Friesland; King of Jerusalem—a mighty king, absolute ruler of an Empire the world had never before seen nor would again.

From Seville on the Guadalquivir, from Oporto, from Corunna and Valencia and Almeria, sailed Spanish ships—small caravels, frail craft, often no more than thirty tons burthen. They sailed prodigious distances. The further they sailed, the more they discovered; the more they discovered, the greater the trading. Such escalation led to an increase in shipbuilding and in the size of ship needed to transport the treasures of the East and West for the benefit of the Spanish Court, the King and his hidalgos. Ship construction still followed traditional lines but ships became longer and broader, lumbering carracks.

The uniformity of rig lasted many years. There were three masts —fore, main and mizzen—which carried a spritsail, foresail and foretopsail, main course, main topsail and a lateen mizzen. Increasing hull dimensions did nothing to further their close-wind sailing characteristics. These were stubby ships, cumbersome hulks, slow to manoeuvre and difficult to handle in stormy weather. Many sailed, never to be heard of again. Disease, starvation, storm, the toll in human lives was a high price to pay for lining the purses of the Dons.

Spanish and Portuguese settlements were established in the New Territories. In 1518 Hernando Cortez led his band of Conquistadores into Mexico, defeated Montezuma and captured Mexico City. Throughout what was to become known as the Spanish New World, fortress settlements were built. The mineral wealth was staggering. Soon more gold was being mined in the Americas in one year than had existed in the whole of medieval Europe. Mountains of silver were discovered. Lima, capital of the Vice-Royalty of Peru, was founded by Francisco Pizarro in 1535. The huge local deposits of silver led to a mint being formed there and produced astronomic loads of coin from 1565 to 1824. The Imperial City of Potosi, founded by Villarrel in 1546, was close to the largest silver mines in South America and its silver production was prodigious throughout the period until 1825.

Such wealth could not remain a secret. All Europe knew of Spain's incredible riches. But her ability to defend her possessions, her merchant ships, her overseas settlements was hopelessly over-stretched. Jealous European nations, such as France and England, cast envious eyes at such enormous wealth bridging the Atlantic and Pacific Oceans. The curtain rose upon a bloody marine history— a new age of piracy began.

There was nothing new about piracy. The Corsairs of Moorish Africa were a known and well-documented hazard of those waters. However, a hypocritical pirate appeared on the scene—a form of hybrid, the privateer. Licensed by his Sovereign to plunder, according to his 'Letters of Marque', there was only a fine hairs-breadth of distinction between his own blood-letting and the cutlass-wielding of his skull and crossbones cousin. In truth, all were pirates yet the value of 'Letters of Marque' must not be under-estimated. If the privateer was ever caught, he could claim the 'Courtesies of War'; the common pirate was simply hanged. Without doubt, the fine distinction sufficed: the pirate was a blackhearted scoundrel hated by all; the privateer acted in the Crown's name and was a patriotic scoundrel. There was, however, no difference between their objectives—to plunder the Spanish of their treasures.

Such navy as England possessed was sold off on Henry VI's death, according to the terms of his will, to settle his debts. It was Elizabeth who, converting private ships to Royal use, commissioned privateers to boost her Treasury, began to put together a Royal Navy of sorts, wooed pirates with Queen's Commissions and saw the same ship's Master become, in turn, pirate, privateer, naval captain, knight.

France was close behind England in the trade of pillaging. In 1537 she raided Honduras and captured nine ships of the treasure fleet. Later, in 1543, she burned the settlement of Cubagua off Venezuela. In 1554 François Le Clerc pillaged Santiago de Cuba;

the following year his lieutenant, Jacques Sores, razed Havana.

Hawkins and his kinsman Drake roamed the Spanish Main, returning to England and Elizabeth with vast treasure spoils. Spain attempted to protect her sea lanes by the institution of armed convoys. Two fleets left Seville each spring, their routes and sailing dates meticulously ordered, as research in archives in Madrid and Seville can testify to this day. One fleet, the Galeones de Tierra Firme, sailed to New Granada for the port of Cartagena. Here the fleet would load gold, pearls and emeralds. At Portobello, it would take on silver from Lima's rich mines.

The second, the New Spain fleet, sailed to Vera Cruz on the Gulf coast of Mexico and loaded silver and coin. Later, it sailed to Panama to pick up spices, porcelain and silk goods of the Orient carried overland from the Pacific port of Acapulco. Both fleets wintered in harbour and made rendezvous at Havana the following March. Together the treasure fleets, Plata Flotas, escorted by men o'war, sailed for Spain. These convoys proved their success in the early years, until the English (and later the Dutch) formed attacking fleets from which no convoy was safe. Yet, sailing in convoy held problems from the start. If the convoy ran into a storm, not one vessel perished but often the entire fleet.

Following the Franco-Spanish alliance, England and, to a lesser degree, the Dutch continued to earn the Spanish King's displeasure. Although actively aided by the Pope, whose Papal Decree in 1570 excommunicated Elizabeth, Philip's demands for the curbing of English privateers received scant attention. In 1572 Drake sailed around the Caribbean with two light, fast moving ships, returning again to England laden with spoils.

Between 1577 and 1580, with three ships, including his beloved *Golden Hind*, Drake sailed through Magellan's strait and sacked the indolent settlements of Spain which slept safely, as they thought, warmed by Pacific waters. Up the coast of Peru, Drake pillaged, and returned after three years with a fortune for his Queen and to a Knighthood for himself. Philip threatened in vain. Throughout Spain's New Settlements, fear laid bare the weakness of Spanish defence. Elizabeth had rejected marriage plans, so Philip began planning his Armada. He would carry the war to England, conquer the upstart heretic Elizabeth and put paid once and for all to the attacks on his settlements and Plata Flotas.

Sir Francis Drake, from an early engraving. (Mansell Collection)

'The Most Fortunate Fleet' sailed for 'the Enterprise of England' from Corunna, on 23 July, 1588. One hundred and thirty-one ships made up this Armada carrying 24,607 soldiers and seamen, commanded by 1,338 generals, colonels, captains and other officers. Gentlemen volunteers totalled 1,549 including artillery officers and some 800 ecclesiastics and other non-combatants. Altogether more than 28,000 men sailed to do their King's will, somewhat reluctantly commanded by the Duke of Medina Sidonia.

In the manner of that day, squadrons of ships had been supplied by various regions of Spain, manned and officered by those same regions. Thus the Duke himself, styled floridly as 'The Captain General of the Ocean Fleet', personally commanded ten galleons and two light zabras—fast, yacht-like vessels used for carrying fleet messages—that comprised the squadron of Portugal; his flagship was the *San Martin*. Second in command was Juan Martinez de Recalde, a fine sailor respected throughout Spain but, more important, loved by his men. His flag was carried in the *Capitana Santa Ana* and he headed the Biscayan fleet of ten galleons and four raiding pataches, or fast, lightly-armed ships.

The squadron of Castile comprised fourteen galleons and two pataches under Don Diego Flores de Valdes, a brilliant sailor but autocratic, jealous and quarrelsome. Philip had made him Chief of Staff to the Duke, much to the consternation of other commanders; their animosity was so apparent that Diego Flores transferred to Sidonia's flagship, there to remain throughout the campaign. The tradition of regional squadrons had much to commend it, although intense rivalry between provinces at times led commanders into situations of tactical imprudence. Bent upon self-glory and personal honour, they disregarded many of the Duke's orders, operating their squadrons with scant regard to the overall plan.

Don Pedro de Valdez was Captain General of the Andalusia squadron of ten ships and two pataches. A similar number of ships made up the Guipuzcoa squadron commanded by Don Miguel de Oquendo. The squadron of the Levant, from Barcelona and Italian ports, also numbered ten ships under the command of Don Martin de Bertendona. The *Santa Maria Encoronada* on which Don Alonso de Leiva, commander of the ground troops and his staff took passage, sailed among this squadron.

Stores, reserve arms and ammunition, field artillery and gun

The sharpest engagement between the English and Spanish fleets on July 25th off the Isle of Wight. (Mansell Collection)

carriages, camp material and wagons, mules, horses and their grooms were all carried in twenty-five hulks—merchantmen with Juan Gomez de Medina in command. A further twenty-two pataches and zabras for reconnoitering and scouting made up a squadron of their own, commanded by Don Antonio Hurtado in his flagship *La Nuestra Senora del Pilar de Saragoza*. Don Diego Medrano commanded four galleys from Portugal and, lastly, Don Hugo de Moncada in the *Capitana San Lorenzo* led four galleasses from Naples, huge vessels bristling with fifty cannon. A galleass was a cross between a galley and a galleon, with a complement of 300 rowers, 300 soldiers and 120 sailors. Much was expected of these four ships should the wind ever drop in the English Channel; they were the *San Lorenzo, Zuniga, Napolitana* and *Girona*.

By July 29 (Spanish Gregorian Calendar), land had been sighted from the crow's nest of the *San Martin*. On July 30 the fleet made its way up-Channel towards Plymouth, noting signal fires being lighted from headland to headland along the English coast. The Armada had been expected and the English were preparing a reception.

Lord Howard of Effingham, Earl of Nottingham, Lord High Admiral of England, took his fleet of eighty ships to sea, behind his flagship *Ark Royal*. At sea, this fleet divided into two columns; Sir Francis Drake as second-in-command was in the *Revenge*. Early dawn of August 1 saw Effingham to the windward of the Spanish fleet, pennants and standards flying, gunports open, guns run out, sails straining as *Ark Royal* led her squadron to attack the Spanish vanguard. Martin de Bertendona's *Regazona* turned with the entire Levant squadron to meet this attack but was thwarted by the swifter moving English and raked by cannon-fire from long-range ordnance. Gunfire rumbled like thunder, echoing across the sea; flying metal tore great holes in the timbers and flung lethal splinters of wood around the decks killing and maiming soldiers and sailors alike and ripping the shrouds to pieces.

Followed by Frobisher in *Triumph* and Hawkins in *Victory*, Drake engaged the enemy's rear-guard on the left flank and severely damaged the Biscayan squadron. At a range of 300 yards the English cannon could pulverise the Spanish without reply as the Armada's cannon, demi-cannon and perriers (capable of firing 16

Lord Howard of Effingham, Admiral of the English Fleet. (Mansell Collection)

and 15 lb shot) were only effective at 150 yards. Again and again the English attacked and then withdrew before coming within range of the Spanish guns.

Towards that afternoon, as the slow-moving ships neared Torbay, the Duke signalled that his fleet should reassemble. Strength of defence lay in numbers and, scattered as his ships were, they would become cut out and easy prey for the fast manoeuvering English. The Armada still intended to sail its ordered way in crescent formation towards its agreed rendezvous with the Duke of Parma to help him cross from Flanders to the coast of Kent. In total confusion, as the Duke's order to assemble was put into execution, the *Santa Catalina* rammed the *Nuestra Senora des Rosario*, capitana of the Andalusian squadron, tearing off her bowsprit and spritsail yard, which in turn brought down her mizzen mast with its rigging and mainyard. Within a few minutes a great ship was hopelessly disabled. Masts and yards, sails and rigging littered her deck and trailed into the sea. Helpless, she drifted along with the wind.

Hardly had this tragedy struck the Spaniards when a shattering explosion was heard and a gout of flame followed by rolling black clouds of smoke was seen issuing from the *San Salvador*. The decks and her after-castle had been blown away in the explosion. On board was the Vice-Admiral of the Guipuzcoan squadron; also on board was a considerable part of the Armada treasure which had been divided between several ships for safety's sake. For two or three hours she burned, well into the gloom of late afternoon. But as the fires dimmed and the *San Salvador* was evidently doomed, many of her chests of coin and other valuables were transferred. Thus abandoned, *San Salvador* was later boarded by Hawkins and reputedly towed into Weymouth Harbour.

Meanwhile, the crippled *Rosario* was left further behind by the Armada. By dawn of the next day she had been boarded by Drake, quickly pillaged of easily moved valuables and towed into Brixham, hence to Dartmouth as a prize, much to the anger of Sir Martin Frobisher who later complained that Drake, under the guise of war, still operated with a pirate's greed. There was an element of truth in this. A reputed 55,000 gold ducats and much gold plate, richly embellished swords and jewellery found its way into Drake's capacious pockets.

Off Portland Bill the two fleets again met in sustained battle, their booming guns blazing fire and smoke. The English once again manoeuvred with greater superiority, used as they were to the Channel winds, the tides and the shoals. For the next two days a mass of confused Spanish galleons wheeled about, time and again, as the English, now formed into four squadrons under Howard, Drake, Hawkins and Frobisher, hunted stragglers, cut out flankers and generally caused mayhem to the slow moving Armada, while the Duke still tried to protect his merchant hulks and supply vessels for the rendezvous with Parma.

Two stragglers, threatened by Hawkins, brought the galleasses of Naples to the rescue, yet this resulted in severe damage to all four vessels. In coming to aid a supply hulk, the galleasses risked more

The English fleet is seen putting out from Plymouth harbour against a south-west wind and its subsequent course is indicated. 'By difficult, patient, precarious tacking the English fleet got to windward . . . and for nine days hung upon the Armada as it ran before the westerly wind up the Channel.' (Mansell Collection)

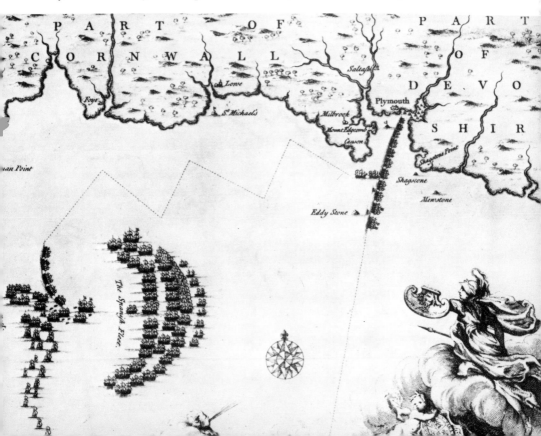

than was proper. Raked again and again by the English, the rowers, chained to their oars, suffered cruelly. *Zuniga* was holed repeatedly by round shot and broke off the engagement, listing heavily. She was never to rejoin the Armada but gained a leeshore, under cover of darkness, where in a small cove in the region of Teignmouth much of her ordnance was jettisoned to bring her higher out of the water for temporary repairs to be made. Biding her time, *Zuniga* crept across Channel to Le Havre for extensive repairs before making her way back to Spain. Of the remaining galleasses *Girona*, *San Lorenzo* and *Neapolitana* were all hit by cannon shot and damaged. The supply hulk *Santa Ana*, the ship that the galleasses had attempted to rescue, was captured by the English after all.

As the Armada slowly sailed through the Dover Strait, the Duke of Medina Sidonia was sorely vexed with the whole endeavour. The English squadrons were sailing rings around his own ships and there was more trouble waiting to greet him—the English Dover squadron of John Seymour's ships and, from the Low Lands, Justin of Nassau and the 'sea beggars'. There was little wonder the Duke had no stomach left for further fighting.

On the night of August 6 Lord Henry Seymour's and Sir Williams Wynter's squadrons joined Howard. Altogether 230 vessels were ready to arraign themselves against the Armada and, as if that were not enough, the weather strongly favoured the English. The Duke decided to anchor at Calais and sent word to Farnese of Parma to join him from Dunkirk and Nieuwpoort to embark his troops in flat bottom barges ready for the invasion of England. Alas for the old Duke, the Armada's position and the weather were ideal for a fireship attack. That night Howard dispatched eight vessels, blazing fiercely, which were quickly swept by wind and tide in a wall of flame toward the Spanish fleet.

The Duke ordered cables to be cut and, at dead of night, in utter confusion, the Armada began fleeing into the North Sea, hopelessly scattered. Dawn of August 8 saw the Armada stretched from Calais to Nieuwpoort. From 8 a.m. to late afternoon the Armada was attacked on all sides.

During the night's confusion, the galleass *San Lorenzo* collided with another ship in shoaling narrows and ran aground, an incredibly rich prize. *San Martin* herself had been holed; more than a hundred direct cannon shot had inflicted terrible damage and dreadful casualties. *San Marco* was foundering; *San Juan de Sicilia* was making much water; *Nuestra Senora de Begona* was barely making way, her shrouds hanging in great shreds. *San Felipe* listed heavily to port. *San Mateo* and *San Juan* of Biscayan origin were both riddled by successive English broadsides and labouring. The *Maria Juan* wallowed, taking in tons of water, settled suddenly and took most of her 300 men with her. And still the wind increased, until a stiff breeze had given way to a near gale.

The Duke of Medina Sidonia knew that survival was most important now. He ordered the remnants of his battered force back to Spain. Their escape route pointed in one direction only, north, around Scotland and then south past the west coast of Ireland thence to Corunna, to disgrace but safety. It was a voyage of terrible ordeal, for so damaged were many that to sail at all would be a feat of endurance. The end of the Armada came in a great suffering of hunger, thirst and pestilence for those who made Spain. For thousands who did not, there was often a horrifying death.

The catastrophe was complete. Out of the proud fleet of 131 ships that set out in July, only 66 returned in September. All along the English, Scottish and Irish coasts lay wrecked Spanish galleons. All along that painful homeward route the sea bed was littered with wreckage. Bodies floated to shore and great chests of coin, gold and silver, chains of gold, plate and goblets both gold and silver, jewellery and ornaments lay scattered on the sea bed. The 'Enterprise of England' was over. All Spain mourned her dead and Philip retired to his gloomy Palace of the Escorial, a broken man.

As each region supplied its ships and men, so it reaped its casualties. The *San Marco* from Portugal was lost somewhere off the coast of Ireland; the *San Felipe* was captured by Justin of Nassau; the *San Mateo* was also captured by the Dutch. The squadron of Castile lost *San Juan*, wrecked on the West Coast of Ireland. *La Trinidad* never returned to Spain, possibly another Irish Coast wreck; *San Juan Bautista* was wrecked off the Blaskets; the patax (or small store ship) *Nuestra Senora del Socorro* was wrecked somewhere on the northern escape.

Those that failed to return home from the Biscay squadron included *El Gran Grin*, wrecked off the coast of county Mayo, and *La Maria Juan*, sunk off the Gravelines north of Dover; the patax *De*

Miguel Suso was another unaccounted ship, lost somewhere on the northern route; the patax *San Antonio de Padua* never returned either, another casualty of the escape. *Santa Maria de la Rosa* was wrecked off county Kerry, Ireland; *San Salvador* blew up in the English Channel and was boarded by the English; *San Esteban* was wrecked off county Clare, Ireland; the urca *Condella* sank after reaching Spain; the patax *La Ascuncion* was lost somewhere off Scotland; the pinaza *Nuestra Senora de Guadelupe* never returned, nor did the pinaza *Magdalena*, sunk or wrecked off Scotland or Ireland.

No squadron suffered more than that from the Levant, which was engaged in the fighting from first to last. Only two galleons returned from Don Martin de Bertendona's gallant fleet. Those that were lost included: *La Lavia* probably wrecked off Ireland; *S. Maria Encoronada*, Don Alonso de Leiva's ship, wrecked in Blacksod Bay, county Mayo; *San Juan de Sicilia* (strong evidence supports the view this casualty is the famous Tobermory wreck); *La Trinidad Valencera* wrecked in Kinnagoe Bay, county Donegal; *La Anunciada*, ripped apart by storms, was scuttled in the mouth of the Shannon river; *San Nicolas Produneli* failed to return to Spain— there is no clue to her disappearance; *Juliana* was lost somewhere off Ireland; *Santa Maria de Vision* never returned, lost somewhere off Scotland or Ireland.

From the squadron of hulks, *El Gran Grifon* was lost off Scotland; *Perro Marino* is considered a doubtful loss; *Falcon Blanco Mayor* was captured by the English; *Castilo Negro* was lost off Ireland; *Barca de Amburg* foundered off Scotland; *San Pedro Mayor*, a hospital ship, was wrecked off South Devon; *San Pedro Menor* never returned, lost somewhere on the escape route; *Falcon Blanco Mediano* was lost off Connemara; *Ciervo Volante* never returned, lost somewhere on the escape route; *Santa Barbara* never returned and there is no knowledge of her wreck; *Santiago* was lost off Ireland; *David* was lost without knowledge.

Of the huge galleasses of Naples, two of the four ships failed to return: *San Lorenzo* ran aground off Calais; *Zuniga*, terribly damaged in Lyme Bay, finally returned to Spain a year later; *Girona*, captained by Fabricio Spinola, was wrecked on Lacada Point and later found by Robert Sténuit.

Of the galleys of Portugal, *Diana* was wrecked at Bayonne.

It was a horrifying list of tragedy, a ghastly toll of life, an almost incalculable loss of material and a diplomatic disaster for the Spanish—a tragedy far reaching in its ultimate effect.

While Philip of Spain rarely left his gaunt Palace of the Escorial, European political intrigue eroded still further the influence Spain once wrought upon numerous nations. For years reliance on the wealth of goods and materials brought to mainland Spain from overseas had maintained a false grandeur of living. The illusion of the times that those high-born should not demean themselves with thoughts of commerce, heightened by the hidalgos' creed of personal honour, was much exaggerated by the cushioning effect that the riches from overseas colonies brought.

The sons and grandsons of courageous and audacious explorers became indolent and apathetic. Foreign wars and conflict and revolt among Spain's many European dependencies began to deplete the Spanish treasury. More and more taxes were levied. Spain's dependence on her overseas possessions became even greater yet Spain lacked the defence force needed to hold on to what was so important to her.

Throughout the late sixteenth and seventeenth centuries Spain was a great power in decline, kept solvent by the mass of wealth that still poured into mainland Spain from overseas. But as Spanish influence in the world at first stagnated and then faltered, other nations—England, France and the Netherlands—began a hectic period of colonization. Another wealthy empire was born—this time a commercial empire. In 1602 the Dutch East India Company was established, the fabled Vereenigde Oostindische Compagnie, the VOC. Six commercial chambers in Holland subscribed twelve million guilders to build boats to trade with the Spice Islands of the East. Furthermore, the States-General of the Seven United Provinces that made up the Netherlands proclaimed its support for the venture—support unparalleled in scope for a purely commercial undertaking.

The six chambers that financed the VOC were Amsterdam, Rotterdam, Delft, Zeeland, Hoorn and Enkhuizen. Between them they supplied seventeen directors to the company, the Heeren XVII. The company prospered rapidly throughout the East Indies and China. From the States-General its powers were enormous and terms of reference included the right (east of the Cape of Good Hope)

A Dutch insignia and buckle crest. A VOC insignia as worn by
a militiaman of the company. The buck crest shows the three Xs of
Amsterdam. These artifacts helped prove the identity of Hollandia
(see chapter 7). (F. E. Gibson)

to colonize, maintain armed forces, set up courts, sign treaties and even to wage war. Where a paper treaty or a chest of coin could not obtain what was wanted, the sword became a final solution. At the height of its vast enterprise towards the late 1600s, the VOC owned 150 merchant ships and forty men o'war. It maintained 10,000 soldiers. Special treaties with native Princes gained special privileges in Sumatra, Malacca, Macassar, Java, Moluccas, Celebes. By cornering the pepper market the Dutch tripled the price of that commodity in Europe. The trade of all types was truly enormous.

A new, busy merchant sailing route was in being. Ships hastily built, poorly crewed, badly officered, inadequately navigated, piled up as shipwrecks throughout the thousands of miles between Northern Europe and the Far East. High as these casualties were, the vast profits that yet remained only encouraged the VOC to quicken their shipbuilding efforts. In 1621 a West India Company was formed and among its aims was 'above all the humbling of the pride and might of Spain'. The Low Lands wars with Spain had inbuilt an abiding hatred of all things Spanish.

Still in convoys, the Spanish time and again lost treasure to organized attacks. One such piece of business took place in 1628 when Piet Heyn, commanding a Dutch privateering squadron, raided a treasure fleet off Havana. Embarked in longboats, his men stealthily boarded the Spanish fleet, drove the treasure ships on to Matanzas Beach and relieved the Spaniards of more than fifteen million guilders' worth of gold. The Dutch treasury gained sorely needed capital, the VOC declared a fifty per cent dividend that year and for Pieter Pieterszoon Heyn there was honour, fortune and revenge, for twice in his lifetime he had been chained to an oar on a Spanish galley.

There were countless shipwrecks in the sixteenth, seventeenth and eighteenth centuries. Lack of adequate charts and inaccurate navigational instruments played their part, together with the shortage of experienced sailing masters in a time of frantic demands for vessels and escalation of shipbuilding. Spanish treasure ships littered the sea bed from the Caribbean to English, Scottish and Irish coasts and throughout the mainland European shores. The Dutch East Indiamen soon began to follow the Spanish in the degree and range of their shipwrecks. Then a third group of wrecks joined the Spanish and Dutch—the English men o'war.

Deep Sea Treasure

From Queen Elizabeth through the reigns of James Stuart, Charles I, II, and Anne, England's Royal Navy grew. In wars against France and Spain a strong navy became England's defence. A wall of oak guarded the English Channel; the blockade of French and Spanish ports proved an economic success. Spanish and French convoys were seized with relish on the high seas. Prizes and prize money were the emoluments that kept the Royal Navy officered and the Treasury satisfied. Press-gangs roamed English ports and English ships for crews.

England was building a large navy and building it well but the ships were overworked. Service in the Atlantic, Pacific, the Mediterranean, the ravages of sun and marine life bored into woodwork and split timber. Each gale took its casualties and a number of fearsome storms took toll of whole fleets. Of all the wrecks of wooden sailing ships caused by a multitude of reasons during the period of the sixteenth, seventeenth and eighteenth centuries, Spanish, Dutch and English merchantmen and men o'war make up the majority, followed to a far lesser extent by Portuguese, French and Scandinavian vessels.

Storms created most of the disasters, often driving ships miles from their intended passage; what survivors there were, very often were unable to give the exact location of a sinking. The result is that details of vessels known to have sunk in certain areas are simply not available. In the fleet records maintained by the Admiralty, or the VOC in Holland, or the Spanish recorders, brief quill-pen comments list the ship name and 'missing' or 'failed to return to port'. Throughout the sailing-ship sea routes all over the world lie the remains, such as they are, of hundreds of ships and somewhere, close to a pile of ballast stones, will be the coin and plate, the ordnance and jewellery. One wreck may well lead to a companion, for on many occasions whole fleets piled up on inhospitable rocks, with valuable cargoes thought lost for ever.

3

Four Hundred Years of Diving

Throughout the world's sailing routes, commercial merchant bridges had brought to Europe commodities highly esteemed by the growing sophistication of Western civilization. From the East came Chinese porcelain, silks, jade, ivory carvings, spices from Sumatra, Java, the Moluccas. From the New World came the silver of Peru and Mexico, Chilean and Brazilian gold, emeralds from New Granada, pearls from Margarita, tobacco, leather, indigo, cocoa. The New Territories, east and west, provided incalculable wealth and a superabundance of cheaply obtained goods on which vast percentage profits could be made. From the early sixteenth century, three hundred years of heavy trading by sailing ships made fortunes for merchant adventurers and shipowners. For three hundred years thousands of cumbersome vessels risked nature's elements, ran the gauntlet in defiance of pirate and privateer, braved hazards of navigation and aggressors during periods of almost endless European conflicts, with the inevitable result of heavy losses by shipwreck and by plunder.

Engulfed by storms, wrecked by poor navigation, inadequate charts, or in fleeing the attentions of buccaneers, sea beggars, or enemy men o'war, the ships sank. In the deep and the shallows, all along the sailing routes in every quarter of the globe, lay sunken treasure but nowhere more than at the Western Approaches to Europe, in the bottleneck of the English Channel, and in the Caribbean.

Of course, the merchants were loath to give up all hope of their cargoes of gold and silver and whatever other valuable merchandise immersion in seawater would not harm. Attempts at salvage were made to recover some of what was lost even in the sixteenth century, and became more concerted with the steady increase in value of what was to be retrieved. The history of diving owes much to this three-hundred-year period of ocean trading.

The mythology of ancient Greece testifies to man's abiding fascination with the marine world. From a thirteenth century French manuscript comes an illustration of Alexander the Great in his underwater observation chamber, in which, legend has it, he descended into the deep in a glass-sided barrel and therein watched a great serpent so large that it took three days to pass!

In the early sixteenth century the Spaniards, wishing to dive in shallow waters, employed slave labour in the form of Indians to do the work for them. These were expert swimmers, trained to hold their breath from three to five minutes underwater. They often worked in relay teams, clasping stones in order to hasten their descent to the bottom. Once there, amid the wreckage, the Indians felt around until they located something of interest and then surfaced with it. If it was too heavy to lift alone, ropes were passed down to be attached to the object. Primitive though this method was, it proved surprisingly successful in the warm, clear waters of the Caribbean. Of course, casualties were high but human life, particularly Indian life, was cheap—the history of Spanish occupation was not particularly renowned for its humane treatment of the indigenous population.

During the 1600s many experiments were conducted to find a method whereby air could be lowered to the shallow sea bed for divers to replenish their supply without surfacing. Crude diving bells (literally, inverted wooden barrels) were weighted and lowered. What scientists there were in New Spain had little, if any, thought for the problems of underwater work for men. It was sufficient to know that the environment was a hostile one and should be avoided if possible. Phenomena such as hydrostatic pressure were unknown.

The human body is a remarkable piece of engineering technology in the environment for which it was designed—namely, to function within the pressure weight of the Earth's atmosphere at a pressure of one atmosphere, or one Bar. At three miles above the Earth, this pressure drops to 0.5 Bar but in the infinitely more hostile sea, water, being far denser than air, produces much more rapid pressure changes with depth. At a depth of only a thousand feet, the pressure roughly equals 30 Bar.

Warriors fleeing from their enemies are often reputed to have gained safety by leaping into ponds and, by cutting hollow reeds, to have remained underwater sustained by air drawn into their lungs through the reed until it was safe to emerge. This tale is just, but only just, plausible. For, due to hydrostatic pressure, a diver three feet under the surface, drawing air through a pipe, must have his lungs expand against a pressure of approximately 0.1 Bar. The human mechanism of breathing is so carefully balanced that this is almost the limit of what is physically possible. At depths greater than three feet the diver needs to be supplied with air at a pressure equal to that at the depth he has reached.

Such anatomical facts were not realized until the late eighteenth century, although it is somewhat surprising to find that as early as the 1680s, during the reign of Charles II, Sir William Phips invented a diving bell in which a diver was placed on the bottom of the River Thames. Indeed, Sir William had gained his knighthood some years earlier by becoming the first successful salvor in the New World.

In 1641 the Spanish galleon *Nuestra Senora de la Concepcion* foundered on the Ambrosia Bank off Hispaniola. The Spanish attempted to recover some of her vast treasure with little success and finally abandoned the attempt. Some forty years later William Phips led an expedition to the wrecksite and, with the help of Indian divers, recovered silver, gold and precious gems worth over £100,000. It was for this exploit, in which the English Crown shared the rewards, that Phips was knighted, and later became Governor of Massachusetts. He never lost his interest in marine salvage, and a medal struck in his honour referred to an early salvage tool and bore the motto: May Thy Hook always be Hanging.

In 1690 Edmund Halley (1656–1742), an English astronomer, improved upon Phips' design and constructed a diving bell of wood, in which the bottom was open to the sea, so that the air in the bell took up the pressure of the water outside. Fresh air could be

John Lethbridge's diving machine, eighteenth century. In it he dived on numerous English, Dutch and Spanish wrecks and recovered £100,000 for his Dutch and English masters. (Devon Association Papers)

lowered in barrels to the bell. A diver then breathed air at his equivalent depth pressure through a tube but his movements were very restricted. It was to all intents and purposes purely a scientific experiment by Halley into pressure. While not particularly well remembered for this experiment, Halley's Comet, an observation he made in 1682, elevated Halley to Professor of Geometry at Oxford and later to Astronomer Royal at Greenwich in 1720.

It is to a Devonian, John Lethbridge, that the honour must go for the development of the world's first successful commercial diving machine. Commercial it certainly was, for in the Parish Register of Woolborough near Newton Abbot is written: '11th December 1759. Buried Mr John Lethbridge, inventor of a most famous diving-engine, by which he recovered from the bottom of the sea, in different parts of the Globe, almost £100,000 for the English and Dutch merchants, which had been lost by shipwreck.'

Such a sum of money is the modern equivalent of £12,000,000. It is enlightening to note where he dived to locate such treasure in the early 1700s: the Isle of May in the West Indies, Porto Santo near Madeira, and at the Cape of Good Hope. Each location entailed a journey of several months. Altogether Lethbridge dived on the wrecks of four English men o'war, five Dutch East Indiamen, two Dutch men o'war, one English East Indiaman, two Spanish galleons and two London galleys.

Five times this enterprising Devonian almost drowned. Often he dived and worked to a depth of sixty feet and, with difficulty, made seventy feet. The description of his diving machine is best made in his own written words:

'My engine . . . made by a cooper in Stanhope Street, London . . . of wainscot perfectly round, about six feet in length, about two foot and a half diameter at the head, and about eighteen inches diameter at the foot, and contains about thirty gallons; it is hoop'd with iron hoops without and within to guard against pressure. There are two holes for the arms, and a glass about four inches diameter, and an inch and a quarter thick, to look thro', which is fixed in the bottom part, so as to be in a direct line with the eye, two air-holes upon the upper part, into one of which air is conveyed by a pair of bellows, both which are stopt with plugs immediately before going down to the bottom. At the foot part there is a hole to let out water. Sometimes there is a large rope fixed to the back or upper part, by which the people above are directed what to do, and under is fixed a piece of timber as a guard for the glass. I go in with my feet foremost and when my arms are got thro' the holes, then the head is put, which is fastened with screws. It requires 500 weight to sink it, and take but 15 pound weight from it and it will buoy upon the surface of the water. I lie straight upon my breast all the time I am in the engine, which hath many times been more than six hours, being frequently refreshed upon the surface by a pair of bellows. I can move it about 12 foot square at the bottom, where I have stayed many times 34 minutes. . . .'

John Lethbridge was a brave, tough old boy, well deserving of his success in material reward and of the fame his diving 'engine' brought him. He was never a scientist but a practical artisan of immense tenacity, single-minded in his determination to bring prosperity to his family, which he did, ending his days in comfort on his estate at Odicknoll in the parish of Kingskerswell, Devon, purchased with monies earned diving around the world.

The problems of hydrostatic pressure remained unsolved for many years. Diving technology progressed slightly with improvements to and innovations on John Lethbridge's diving 'engine' but it was not until 1823 that air was supplied under pressure to a diver in a successful and practical form. In that year, two brothers from Whitstable in Kent, John and Charles Deane, patented an 'Apparatus to be worn by persons Entering rooms filled with Smoke etc.' This equipment consisted of a helmet with view-ports, a breastplate and a jacket which could be tied around the waist and wrists to exclude 'the smoke or foul air'. A pump for supplying air to the helmet was also described in the patent specification.

It occurred to the brothers that this equipment would also work under water. To this end, John Deane, appropriately clad, entered the sea and almost drowned because the weight of his helmet turned him upside down. He quickly added lead-soled boots to keep himself the right way up and these became the standard equipment for 'hard-hat' divers, as they became known.

John Deane used his diving suit to explore the wrecks of the *Royal George* and *Mary Rose* off Spithead and aroused considerable interest by retrieving and offering for sale numerous artifacts from these wrecks. An artist's drawing, compiled from Deane's underwater descriptions, hangs in Southsea Castle Museum depicting Deane working on the *Royal George*.

The circumstances of her sinking were extraordinary. On August 29, 1782, the three-deck 108-gun *Royal George*, flagship of Admiral Kempenfelt, was completing the loading of stores prior to sailing with a British fleet for the relief of besieged Gibraltar. Many relatives and friends were on board for their farewells. *Royal George* was anchored in calm water in Spithead Roads receiving stores by lighter. A contemporary eyewitness, a crew-member, reported to the subsequent enquiry: 'there was a bodily crack and she began to roll over on her portside, hesitated a moment and then sank.' More than 800 men, women and children had been on board. Within

Ready to go below. Standard suit diving is a team affair. The diver relies on his air from those above. (Captain T. A. Hampton Collection)

minutes boats from Portsmouth and Southsea were on the scene, but only 300 were rescued. Admiral Kempenfelt perished with his ship. It was a tragedy long remembered in Portsmouth.

By 1840, a German immigrant to England, Augustus Siebe, having worked along similar lines to John Deane, fully demonstrated the usefulness of their equipment when the Royal Navy decided that the wreck of the *Royal George* was a hazard to shipping. A team of Royal Engineers were trained to use the new equipment and successfully broke up the wreck. For the first time the importance of the diver as an underwater worker was impressed upon the Admiralty.

Equipment based on Siebe's original designs became the mainstay of hard-hat diving until the Second World War. The firm of Siebe Gorman is still well-known today as developers and makers of diving equipment. But the problems of pressure at increasing depths remained to be solved. Siebe's equipment of the middle 1800s restricted the diver to a depth of a hundred feet for working purposes. Below this depth the human body was subjected to unacceptable pressure stresses. Pioneer divers, on surfacing rapidly, would suffer from decompression sickness, now more widely known as the 'bends'.

Medical tests revealed that when the body is exposed to compressed air, the air is absorbed into the tissues and the bloodstream. Like a soda siphon containing water and carbon dioxide, the gas dissolved is not in evidence until the pressure is released. The fierce bubbling of soda water may be a pleasantly familiar sight; not so pleasant are the similar, if less violent, bubbles of gas released in the diver's bloodstream if he returns to normal pressure too soon. Bubbles in the bloodstream affect the normal workings of the body. At worst they can cause paralysis or death, at best excruciating pain.

To avoid such a danger divers working at depths below thirty feet have to ascend slowly, the time taken to decompress being commensurate both with depth and duration of dive. As a result of practical experience and research, decompression tables were drawn up for the diver's protection. As an example, a diver working for twenty minutes at a depth of a hundred feet would need a decompression time of ten minutes at depths of both thirty and fifteen feet.

Although the decompression problem was recognized and basic-ally understood by the turn of this century, further problems emerged as divers wished to explore greater depths. At 150 feet experienced divers would act strangely, failing to carry out their work properly and with scant regard for their own safety, giving the appearance of intoxication. The divers themselves referred to this with some eloquence as 'the raptures of the deep' but it was nothing to joke about and many lives were lost. The cause was discovered in the 1920s. Nitrogen, when under pressure, affected the nervous system, causing 'nitrogen narcosia'.

The modern answer to this problem is to supply the diver with a breathing gas not containing nitrogen. Pure oxygen, however, would not serve the purpose because that, too, becomes poisonous when breathed under pressure. The answer was a helium-oxygen mixture known more commonly as 'heliox', with the proportion of oxygen being reduced with increasing depth.

Modern experience of deep diving with self-contained breathing apparatus to depths of 200 feet has revealed that even with helium mixes the narcotic effect of gas under pressure is not completely eradicated. Every deep-working diver currently uses helios, a light gas easy to breathe but scarce and expensive. Because the speed of sound in helium is different from that in air, the resonant frequency of the voice box is increased. The diver's voice takes on the charac-teristics of Donald Duck, and a complex electronic voice processor is required in order to maintain normal speech sounds.

Diving at 200 feet, however, added more problems. The decom-pression time, after a dive of sixty minutes or so, begins to exceed the working length of the dive, 220 minutes. At the present practical limit of depth, 600 feet, this means that a ten-minute working period would require an impossible eighteen-hour decom-pression time. To allow the diver to work commercially at depth a system of prolonged atmosphere pressurization is employed. This is the modern method of deep sea diving.

At the beginning of a work period, the diver enters pressurized living quarters on the surface. His move to the sea bed is accom-plished by transferring into a submersible decompression chamber which is lowered to the required depth. There, the pressure inside the chamber equals the pressure outside. He can open the chamber door and complete his work schedule. Then, returning to his chamber, he returns to the surface and transfers back, still under pressure, to his living quarters. The diver can remain in these conditions for periods of several days or, if necessary, weeks.

After exposure to pressure for a long time, the blood and tissue become saturated, reaching a condition where no more gas can be absorbed. Provided the pressure is maintained, there is no adverse effect on the diver, except that decompression time is increased. Since decompression can be carried out at the end of a diver's sojourn in pressurized quarters instead of at the end of each dive, he can increase his active working time underwater. Such technical knowledge owes much to space research. However, diving technology back in the 1920s developed very much on the hit or miss-principle.

Before the advent of self-contained breathing gear, atmospheric diving suits were designed to protect the wearer from the pressure of the water, as a means of enabling divers to avoid the problems of having to breathe compressed air. The engineering difficulties were formidable; the suit had to be strong enough to withstand enormous forces at depth yet have limbs sufficiently flexible for the diver to move about and work.

Joseph Peress designed ball and socket type joints for the limbs, which offered the diver the greatest ease of movement. He separated the ball and socket with a fluid 'cushion' contained in a flexible sac, rather like a human joint. The first such suit was built in 1924 and successfully tested. A second unit was built in 1930 in response to salvage companies who wished to recover sunken treasure from deep waters inaccessible to divers at that time.

Both Joseph Peress and his chief mechanic, Jim Jarratt, demonstrated the atmospheric suit on a number of occasions and Jarratt's exploits quickly gained the suit the name of 'Jim'. The inventor's claims for its capabilities were fully justified. In 1934, a depth of 500 feet was achieved. The following year Jim Jarratt dived to identify the wreck of the *Lusitania* off Southern Ireland, lying at a depth of 300 feet.

Wearing SCUBA equipment, Colin Gregory heads for the surface with treasure from the Romney *from over a hundred feet below.* (Benbow/Morris Collection)

For a number of years 'Jim' was virtually 'mothballed' until oil exploration rekindled the suit's usefulness. At the present time ten 'Jims' are working in various parts of the world, often diving to depths of 1500 feet. But for obvious reasons the cost of a 'Jim' atmospheric suit is such that only huge companies can afford to operate such apparatus.

A revolutionary piece of equipment was needed to explore the shallows down to 200 feet or so with complete freedom of movement. In 1943, a French Naval Captain, Jacques-Yves Cousteau, with a colleague, Emile Gagnan, an engineer, perfected a completely Self-Contained Underwater Breathing Apparatus (SCUBA) which was easy to use and cheap to manufacture. This equipment eventually brought underwater exploration within the grasp of thousands of enthusiastic divers throughout the world.

Cousteau named it the Aqua-lung. The diver's breathing gas, compressed air, was carried on his back; the heart of the equipment, the demand valve, ensured that he received air at the correct pressure. The demand valve contains a flexible diaphragm which senses the pressure of the water at the diver's depth; it also releases air from his cylinder or shuts it off according to whether he is inhaling or exhaling. When he exhales, the spent air is released into the water.

At last the coastal sea bed could be explored. By the 1960s the now-familiar black-suited diver, equipped with massive flippers on his feet and air-cylinders upon his back, was systematically surveying the likely areas for traces of old shipwrecks—it was a time for some exciting discoveries. The treasure hunt could truly commence.

4

Kip Wagner and the Plata Flota

The story against which all modern day treasure hunters measure their efforts is undoubtedly that of the 1715 Plata Flota commanded by General Juan Esteban Ubilla and discovered nearly 250 years later by Kip Wagner. Often just referred to as 'the big one', this wreck site inspired European divers to enter the world of treasure hunting and, throughout the United States, successive generations of divers cite this successful episode as the one story above all others that excited their interest in a world beneath the sea.

In July, 1715, ten vessels awaited orders to sail for Spain from Havana—a Plata Flota of quite incredible riches. Five of the galleons, commanded by General Antonio de Echeverz, were heavily laden with South American treasure, gold, emeralds and pearls from Cartagena, Colombia, and silver from Peru loaded at Portobello. The other five galleons, commanded by General Juan Esteban Ubilla, carried 2,300 chests of newly minted coin from Mexico City; Veracruz also had supplied a fortune in gold coins as well as fragile, wafer-thin porcelain from China, together with silks and a quantity of unique, hand-carved jewel-encrusted brooches, bracelets and necklaces ordered by Philip V for a new bride, Elizabeth of Farnese, the young Duchess of Parma. An eleventh vessel was the French ship *Grifon*, which had asked for convoy protection and had received permission to sail with the Flota. The

Kip Wagner examines coins brought up from wrecks of Spanish galleons. (Associated Press)

previous year's Plata Flota sailing had been postponed; hence, the Flota of 1715 was inordinately rich. The treasure amounted to fifty million dollars in modern values.

Such a fleet would have an overall commander—in this case it was Ubilla—and a second-in-command—this was Antonio de Echeverz. Therefore, Ubilla's flagship took the accustomed 'Capitana' position with de Echeverz leading a second division of five galleons as 'Almiranta'. This point is made because, throughout Spanish recorded history, foreign researchers often make the mistake of recording the Capitana or Almiranta as an actual vessel. Commanders of Spanish fleets were always military men, generals in the case of Ubilla and de Echeverz. Command was an overall term; neither was actually involved in sailing or navigating the fleet. Sailing Masters were employed for such purposes. So the terms 'Captain-General' and 'Admiral-General', curious to the uninitiated, have a particular reference for Spanish records. Their poor clerks, handwriting all the records, can surely be excused the abbreviation Almiranta when referring to de Echeverz's flagship, rather than the full Almiranta Nuestra Senora de Rosario y San Francisco Xavier. Thus, through the passage of time and in translating the difficult curls of Castillian/Latin script, do ships' names differ from one narrative to another.

The fleet weighed anchor on Wednesday, 24 July, 1715. As a faint breeze reluctantly filled their sails, the ships slowly made a passage through Havana Roads into the open sea, heading north by east, making for the Cape of Floridas and the Bahama Passage before turning due east for Spain. All along this first part of the voyage lay dangerous reefs and shoals, yet it was an established course with which all Plata Flotas were familiar, dictated by the prevailing winds.

With peace prevailing between England and Spain, Ubilla would have had no fears of English privateers. Only the weather would have been of particular concern to him, considering the value of the treasure he carried, and his anxious eyes would have looked for signs of changing pressure. Perhaps he was aware of an old Caribbean jingle warning of the dangers of hurricanes in those waters:

June too soon;
July stand by;
August, come they must;
September remember;
October, all over.

It was past the warning time, hurricanes were due. But if he could get his fleet through the Bermuda Narrows his passage to Spain would be assured. He was not to be so lucky.

On Tuesday 30, a hot humid day heralded bad things to come. The sea was glassy, the wind stirred the sails intermittently and then died away. First it came from the south and then the west, changing direction constantly. Old seamen could read such signs. A hazy indistinct yellow blob of a sun confirmed that they were in for a severe blow. By mid-afternoon the sea had steepened. Crestless swells caused the galleons to pitch and roll. Leaden canvas hung at the yards. From the north-west black clouds appeared on the horizon and sudden squalls raced across the sea, ripping the surface apart in flurries of white water.

Already the fleet was past Cape Florida and into the Bermuda Narrows; lack of sea-room was an additional hazard. Each sailing master prepared as best he could. Hatches were secured, spritsail and fore and main tops were furled, so too was the mizzen-lateen; main yards were reefed and deck cargo hastily roped down. In typical fashion the wind spiralled around, first from the Nor'West and then settling into a Nor'Nor'East blow. The gale struck the fleet with a sudden fury, heeling each galleon on its beam. The wind vibrated and whipped at the halyards and shrouds and the power of the storm increased until, at night, a full-scale hurricane was driving the separated fleet before it, towards the reefs of the Bermuda Narrows that lay in wait just south of Cape Canaveral.

Reef after reef claimed the galleons. Coral and rock ripped out the bottoms of the heavy laden vessels, helpless in the tumultuous seas. They spilled out their treasures as giant timbers split and masts and rigging crashed down. Within a few minutes nothing but wreckage remained of ten fine galleons. Over a thousand men died in the storm; only a handful lived to report the loss and to describe in harrowing detail the last hours of the treasure fleet of General Juan Esteban Ubilla (in the records of the Mission of the Indies, Seville).

Details of the catastrophe were sent to Seville and to Havana, where Don Juan de Hoyo Solorzano set sail with several sloops and arrived at the wreck-site six months after the great storm. Salvage operations were commenced and Solorzano set up camp on a beach nearest to the wrecks. More than 280 Indians were employed to dive and recover what they could and, although it took time, a total of four million pesos' worth was loaded upon a ship and sent back to Havana. Still, the salvage operation continued. But word of the Spanish treasure fleet's loss spread about the Caribbean and reached the ears of an English privateer.

Captain Henry Jennings had retired to Virginia when, two years previous to the Ubilla wreck, the Treaty of Utrecht had been signed and had established peace between England and Spain. He was, to all intents and purposes, a redundant privateer. But the divide between privateering and piracy was so thin that the lure of Spanish gold tempted Jennings to cross it. Utrecht was a long, long way from Virginia, whilst Sebastian Inlet and Florida were too close to ignore.

Jennings put together a fleet of five small ships with 300 men and raided the Spanish camp set up on the beach. They overwhelmed sixty guards at a storehouse and looted almost 500,000 pesos of silver. Deciding that he was suited to the life of a pirate, Jennings made for Port Royal, there to skirmish and scavenge for a further three years. He then took the King's Pardon, offered to any pirate who surrendered, and retired again to Bermuda, living out his life in total respectability.

The remains of Ubilla's fleet remained further unmolested. The Spanish gave up hopes of recovering any more treasure and, as the years rolled by and successive storms layered the wrecks still further in sand, weed and rock, all traces of Solorzano's beach camp were buried. Scrub grew up on the deserted dunes. For 240 years wind and tide covered the evidence of the disaster.

When Kip Wagner began to take an interest in the area, he soon learnt how quickly the topography of the beach could change. A sudden storm could cover up old landmarks and expose new rocks and reefs overnight. Land was scoured from one location to be piled up on another. After one storm Wagner noticed that a once familiar path, known well for more than six months, had completely disappeared—so, too, had more than fifteen feet of sand bluff. It was hardly surprising that occasionally this desolate shoreline exposed some of its secrets.

Local folklore related that coins in their hundreds had been turning up for many, many years. After the discovery of the first coins, Wagner began regularly to comb the beach and discovered several more oxidised, blackened coins, usually worn thin with age. In most cases the date was just discernible and no coin was dated later than 1715. The discovery, one day, of a bright, mint-condition

Gold and silver from the depths. A handful of treasure, pieces-of-eight, crowns, reis and guineas—coins of history. (Benbow/Morris Collection)

piece-of-eight stamped with the Jerusalem Cross on one side and the Spanish arms of Leone and Castille on the other confirmed his determination to become a serious hunter of sunken treasure.

Wagner already had enough coins to point to the significance of the date 1715, and an expert numismatist, Robert Nesmith, confirmed that '. . . the coins were the most important finds from a Spanish Plate Fleet ever made in Florida, both historically and numismatically.' Wagner and a friend, Dr Kip Kelso, read every book they could lay their hands on, in libraries as far afield as Miami, Tampa, Jacksonville and Washington D.C. The University of Florida also helped and, piece by piece, the two men built up the story of Ubilla's treasure fleet and so found the reference to Solorzano's fortified beach camp established for the salvage operations.

In the process, they learnt one of the golden rules of historical research, to hold fast to what they truly believed in the search for proof, and not to be swayed by opinion backed merely by academic qualification. Wagner sent one of his coins to the Smithsonian Institute and asked if it could have come from Ubilla's Plata Flota. Back came the courteous reply, that such a thing was impossible as the fleet had gone down 150 miles further south in the Florida Keys. It was an intense disappointment for Wagner and Kelso. But the bug of discovery was upon them both. They were sure that there was a significance in the dates of the coins, and they were equally sure that it was quite possible to be mistaken as to the whereabouts of a fleet of sailing ships that sank 240 years ago. Kelso went to Washington D.C. to research in the archives of the Library of Congress. A considerable part of successful treasure hunting stems from individual checking. And a considerable part of the final satisfaction comes from proving oneself right and other people wrong. The treasure hunter must be single-minded in his application.

Kelso became boggle-eyed from hours of reading but he stumbled across the writings of an English cartographer, Bernard Romans, who had written in 1775:

> *Directly opposite the mouth of San Sebastian River*
> *happened the shipwreck of the Spanish Admiral who was*
> *the Northernmost wreck of fourteen galleons and a hired*
> *Dutch ship, all laden with specie and plate. . . .*

Kelso was elated. The document seemed to back Wagner's theory and there was more to follow. As Kelso was about to return the book, he noticed a drawing on the flyleaf. Romans had very kindly drawn a detailed map and, nearly two hundred years later, Kelso could distinguish and recognize the coastline drawn. Near the outlets of Sebastian Inlet and Indian River had been written: 'Opposite this river, perished the Admiral commanding the Plate Fleet of 1715, the rest of the Fleet were wrecked between this and the Bleech Yard'. It was at this point that Wagner's historical reading paid a dividend; he realized that this must be an area near the mouth of St Lucie River, flat and open, with ample fresh water, where salt-encrusted sails could be washed and 'bleeched dry in the sun stretched full upon the grass'.

It was logical that Solorzano's beach camp would be close to the salvage operations. 'Find the camp-site,' thought Wagner, 'and I'm within spitting distance of the wrecks themselves.' Wagner accordingly bought a second-hand mine detector for fifteen dollars and extended his searches to include any likely looking hollow or dell above high water mark. Up to now this unlikely searcher for sunken treasure had not put a toe in the sea. Nor did he, until he found Solorzano's camp.

Half-a-mile north of his usual beach, the mine detector began whining away and Wagner dug up a ship's bronze spike and a cannon ball. He charted the periphery of perhaps half-an-acre with his detector and uncovered clumps of cannon balls that surely marked gun sites, although the cannons obviously had been removed. He was convinced that this was the camp-site and was determined to begin serious investigations from that point.

Early diggings revealed pieces of broken earthenware, which were painstakingly pieced together where possible by Mrs Wagner. Family and friends were at first press-ganged and then readily volunteered their help. A pair of cutlasses with blades half rusted away turned up beneath a few inches of sand; silver scraps of molten metal were next. Then followed a discovery that stopped everybody in their tracks and brought home the fantastic possibilities and potential value of what might be discovered. Wagner found a gold ring.

It was no ordinary ring, for it was set with a large diamond of two-and-a-half carats and set around the main stone were six others, approximately half a carat each. The ring was valued at $20,000. From that moment Wagner was really hooked into both aspects of the treasure: the historical attraction—an all-consuming passionate desire to learn more of eighteenth century marine life— and the intrinsic value of the treasure itself; to handle coins that pirates and privateers fought over, to gaze again upon the fabled piece-of-eight, the dubloon, escudo and the rest of these highly romanticized coins, well documented in fact and fiction.

It is testimony to Wagner's philosophy that he admitted to his material interest and concern as well as to his historical curiosity. The inherent honesty of Wagner's character was such that he never dallied with the humbug of many so-called marine archaeologists who declare, hand on heart, that they are only interested in historic artifacts, not in treasure. People will always be attracted to sunken treasure and the greater the material rewards, the more fulfilling the satisfaction of accomplishment.

At times, Wagner's sole companions in his survey of the camp-site were flocks of pelicans wheeling down as if to check on his latest diggings. It was this that gave Wagner the idea of an aerial survey of the immediate sea area off the beach. At a local airfield he hired a small aircraft. But what should he look for? Wooden vessels wrecked over two hundred years ago would no longer bear any resemblance to the outline of a ship. Only ballast stones or cannon might show up. It took a little time to adjust to the fresh perspective but, when passing over Palmar de Ais, Wagner spotted a long dark area showing on the sea bed; from the darkness rows of finger-like objects protruded at differing angles. The dark mass could well be ballast stones; the fingers could equally well be cannon. It was time, at last, for Wagner to get wet.

With his pilot friend, Wagner launched a skiff through the surf and located the sea bed position as seen from the air. With face-masks on, both men dived into the clear October water. Within minutes they were gazing down on heaps of rounded ballast stones. Wagner swam lower—the whole wreck site was no deeper than twenty feet—and there he saw his first cannon, wrapped in a lime green crust, embedded with shells and, attached to the muzzle, waving in the current, a few strands of bright green seaweed. Eighteen cannon were counted in all. No timber could be seen, sand enveloped the edge of the ballast stones; some of them were more

Ciné-filming is growing as an aid to wreck site recording. The camera housing is a pressure chamber tested to 250 feet and weighted for balance. Better quality film now available will lead to an extension of this aid for nautical archaeology. (Dave Burrell)

than fifty pounds in weight. It was quite a moment for the one-time building contractor.

Wagner's business sense dictated his next moves. He would need a team of divers to help him, a boat and legal protection from modern pirates. Personnel were hand-picked, people he knew and could trust. From a surplus store he bought a forty-foot Navy Liberty launch and christened it *Sampan*. From the trustees of the Florida Improvement Fund—the body that controls the recovery of sunken treasure, among its many other responsibilities—he obtained a licence to dive and recover wreck items. The State of Florida would be entitled to twenty-five percent of the proceeds. Having settled in part some of the business details, Wagner cast around for a name and hit on the Real Eight Co. Inc., from Ocho Reale, or piece-of-eight.

Wagner's first crew consisted of a team of eight friends: Dr Kip Kelso, who became curator, translator and librarian; Colonels Dan Thompson and Harry Cannon (an aptly named diver), both from the Patrick Air Force Base, headquarters of the Atlantic Missile Range; an ex-Navy diver, Louis Ullian, who undertook the duties of chief technician for salvage equipment; Lisbon Futch, an experienced seaman of local waters and shoals, who skippered the *Sampan*; Delphine Long and Erwin Taylor, two other expert boat handlers; lastly, a banker, C. R. Brown, to act as business consultant. A little later two additional men from the rocket range augmented the diving team, Captain John Jones and Warrant Officer Robert Johnson.

In preparation for salvage, Wagner had bought air hoses for shallow water diving; suction air hoses, extra marker buoys, haul-up baskets equipped with hand lines and a bulky boarding ladder. At first and quite understandably the enthusiasm of the divers ran away with cold reason and they finned their way below the surface in a highly disorganized catch-as-catch-can type of search. But once they had all grown accustomed to the scene below, Wagner was able to get them to work quickly and thoroughly in a more organized fashion.

Sand on the sea bed was churned up by ceaseless swells, limiting visibility. As one surge came in, divers anchored themselves by clinging on to ballast stones; the return flow sent their bodies pointing in a fresh direction, feet swinging with the current. This was strangely disorienting at first, although the divers soon grew used to the phenomenon. A work pattern evolved through trial and error. At least the shallow water saved them the problems of working under pressure at depth. Provided they had enough air, it was possible to spend hours below surface. They made a careful examination of the ballast stone rockpile and staked out the area in metal grid squares, mapping cannon, stones and sand overburden. As items were found by the removal of ballast stones, their grid positions were marked before they were retrieved. Brown earthenware potsherds were the first finds and the Florida State Museum at Gainsville welcomed them with excitement. Then Lou Ullian came up with six blackened pieces-of-eight. That day saw eleven coins retrieved. It was obvious that the passage of years had deposited a huge amount of sand over parts of the wreck. By utilising a water pump on board *Sampan*, a hose and a long pipe, a suction pump was created which worked very well, clearing a channel of sand in which a more careful examination could be made. Here, original wood frames were discovered, pulpy and disintegrating into a black cloud of debris that streamed away with the surging currents.

Wedges of blackened silver were found. The copper used in refining silver oxidises into a thin black coating and is quite easily removed by electrolytic action in a solution of zinc and caustic soda. The metal on the surface is usually tainted but, beneath, coins can be found preserved bright and in the same condition as when first lost. These silver wedges fitted the shape of a barrel or small keg capable of being carried by hand—perhaps a 100 lb load.

Interesting artifacts were discovered daily: a silver cup, a fork, a sounding lead and then, one day, Dan Thompson surfaced, grabbed a nylon rope and shouted, 'When I tug on the rope, you all pull.' Up from the sea bed came a greenish-black mass. Wagner caught hold of a piece which broke off in his hands and there, revealed under the black surface, were hundreds of bright silver coins, about 50 lb weight of them. Thompson went below again, this time with Harry Cannon, and twice more they surfaced, each time with only slightly smaller clumps of coin. The 'M' mark on these coins testified to the Mexico City mint.

Valuable finds continued so long as diving and the good weather lasted. Their coin totals were now into the hundreds and it was a happy band of Real-Eighters that recognized that the approaching bad weather would call a halt to their underwater activities for a few weeks. In fact, one storm period lasted a good two months but it was during this enforced inactivity that Kip Wagner made a most fantastic find—or rather, to put the record straight, his nephew Rex Stocker did.

Wagner had all the time continued his habit of beachcombing after storms or high winds, taking his nephew with him. It was on one of those searches, while Wagner paced along the shore and the teenager looked along a high sand bluff behind, that Rex suddenly shouted and ran towards Wagner, a glittering gold chain wrapped around his arm. To be exact, it was eleven feet four-and-a-half inches of gold chain, 2,176 separate flower-shaped links weighing altogether half-a-pound. The chain held a pendant in the shape of a dragon, the size of a man's thumb. From its belly opened a gold toothpick; the tail formed an ear-cleaning spoon and its half-opened mouth formed a whistle. It was an Oriental form of admiral's chain of office, greatly admired by the Spanish. Records exist of a similar object given to the Duke of Medina Sidonia by Philip II at the beginning of the 1588 Armada.

The chain was a magnificent find—and not even from the sea. It seemed incredible that such a fragile, gloriously worked piece of art should survive so many years. If Wagner needed any confirmation that the wrecks would release marvellous treasure, this artifact convinced him that there were still many surprises in store. The gold dragon and chain were valued by experts at between $40,000 and $60,000. They were exactly right. At a New York auction the dragon was sold for $50,000.

When diving could begin again, a daily succession of finds came

Gold chains, identical with those seen in portraits of Renaissance gentlemen. The one on the outside is about 2.5 metres long and weighs over four pounds. These were found in Girona. (Ulster Museum)

up: a cannon, another gold chain eight feet five inches in length from which hung a gold pendant with miniature portraits encased in glass, a silver crucifix, a ship's bell, some intact earthen jars and then came their first gold coin. It was a thick, heavy eight-escudo piece, in brilliant mint condition, every segment of the Royal Shield of Arms of Philip V clear and perfect. Gold does not tarnish in salt water but comes to the surface pristine and welcoming as the day it was lost. The coin bore the inscription 'Philip V by the Grace of God, 1714.' The letter 'M' denoted the Mexico City mint; 'J' that of the Ensayador, Jose Eustaquio de Leon; the Roman numeral 'VIII' was its value of eight escudos—a splendid coin that fetched a regal price at auction of $10,000. It was a well-remembered day because, by the end of it, seven more bright gold coins lay in Wagner's hand.

Gold ingots were also found. One weighed seven-and-a-half

Gold chains and 'sweetheart' rings are the sad evidence of the human side of shipwreck. From a French or Spanish wreck in the Vigo area.

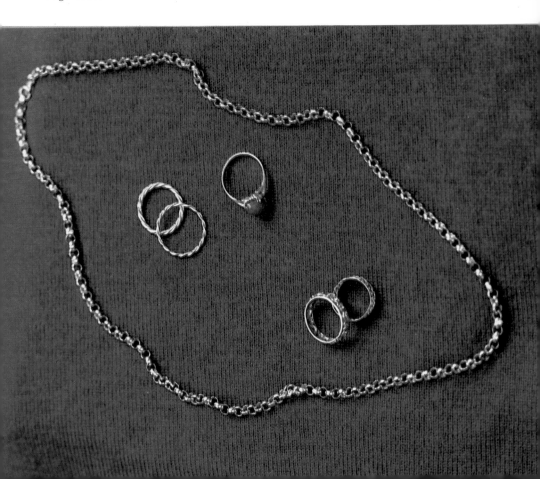

pounds and was sold for $17,500. As the work continued on other wrecks of Ubilla's ill-fated fleet, the record of finds began to read like the contents of an Aladdin's cave. Wagner himself was underwater when he noticed the sand dredger throwing out pieces of white and blue pottery. Quickly he tapped the operator's shoulder and switched off the suction. Together they looked at an exposed wall of trench, a surface of mud or clay and, studded in the substance, plainly to be seen, pieces of porcelain. Wagner used his fingers carefully to prise out intact cups and bowls of Chinese art. On the surface Wagner instructed everyone not to touch the trench until he had checked out the find. Dr Kip Kelso soon obliged. The porcelain was wafer-thin K'ang-Hsi porcelain, miraculously intact because it had been packed in its own clay. For days on end careful excavation revealed and brought to the surface marvellous examples of Chinese work. It was a labour of love for Mrs Wagner to piece together some of the broken objects.

Porcelain, gold, silver, the wrecks were giving up their long-held treasures. The amount of work to be done was enormous. So Kip Wagner brought in further help, this time a professional salvage crew from California, Mel Fisher and his experts. As the months rolled by so the list of treasure grew. Some days were truly memorable, like the one on which Fisher, using a high-pressure excavating hose, uncovered a trench fifteen feet long and six feet wide neatly carpeted by 1,033 gold dubloons. Another day uncovered a hoard of 200 four- and eight-escudo pieces.

The range and value of recovered items soared: a number of silver wedges, thousand upon thousand silver coins in varying condition (one lead-lined, once-wooden, chest contained, fused together, three thousand silver pieces-of-eight), a gold dragon pendant, gold chains, gold jewel boxes, intact K'ang-Hsi porcelain, thousands of gold coins, gold discs, pewter plates, silver forks, gold rings, silver candlesticks, tankards, anchors, cannon and a whole host of historic artifacts. Kip Wagner's Florida treasure soon mounted up to more than $5,000,000.

Unfortunately, Wagner was not to survive to see the final work but he left behind an example of modesty, dogged perseverance and patient application, an example that was soon to be taken up on the other side of the Atlantic by Roland Morris, Robert Sténuit, Rex Cowan and many others.

5

The Wreck of the Association

Geoff Upton and David Regalado, members of the Roland Morris team, made ready to dive below the Gilstone Rock, staggering slightly as their boat pitched in the usual swell experienced so often at the Western Rocks in the Scillies. Like a sentinel, Bishop's Rock Lighthouse stood tall and near, silently watching, a lick of white water at its base. On his last dive Doug Rowe thought he had spotted a bronze cannon, now Geoff and Dave were to attempt to locate it and to strap a small buoy around its muzzle. Roland Morris was anxious to identify the wreck as the *Association*, for it was on that vessel he held a Ministry of Defence agreement to dive and work. But identification was of paramount importance to stop rival diving teams poaching. A cannon could well provide the necessary identification.

'Here, at the end of the gully, that's where I saw it, muzzle up,' Doug's stubby fingers traced along an underwater map he had drawn. He glanced at both divers, 'Do you think you can find it?'

'Sure', answered Geoff, 'I know exactly where you mean.'

Within minutes Geoff and Dave were finning below, diving down between granite cliffs and back towards the gully Doug had drawn, between the outer and inner ledges of the Gilstone. It was an awesome place, south-west of St Agnes Island, in among countless reefs

LE.COMTE.DE
VERMANDOIS

and part-submerged rocks. It did not require much of an imagination to visualize the horror of becoming wrecked in that savage area of the Scillies.

With the weather doing its best to make life difficult topsides, it was a relief for Geoff and Dave to be below, away from the surface chop. They saw the bronze cannon Doug had spotted and another and a third; they strapped marker buoys around all three, took measurements and surfaced but not empty-handed. They took up with them an iron cannon ball encrusted with sea-growth. When cracked open it revealed the broad arrow mark of the Royal Navy— a piece of the jig-saw towards identification.

By the divers' descriptions Roland Morris deduced that the ordnance was nine or ten feet in length and would weigh about three tons. He decided to obtain a trawler, fit a bow-lift on her and retrieve the cannon in that way. Again the weather caused delay and the Morris team became increasingly anxious about the possible effect of the constantly changing sea bed. Would they ever find the cannon again? Patience is a virtue much required by those who aim to recover lost items from the sea, for the deep gives up its treasures reluctantly.

At last a day dawned clear and relatively calm and not a second was wasted in getting below to re-locate the first cannon and to attach the trawler's wire-rope to nylon straps. Carefully the great cannon was lifted just below the trawler's keel. There it was secured for the trip back to St Mary's and Hugh Town Quay where a waiting army of holidaymakers welcomed Roland Morris, his team and the cannon.

It proved to be a marvellously adorned and embellished cannon— but a *French* culverine. The cannon had been cast in honour of le Comte de Vermandois, after the custom of the day, and it was unquestionably French. Roland Morris reflected on the clues the wreck site had so far provided. A gold Portuguese 4,000 Reis of 1706, an English broad-arrow-marked cannon ball and now a

The Arms of the Comte de Vermandois. A French bronze cannon seized by the British after the battle of Vigo Bay, mounted on board Association *and finally brought back to the surface by the Roland Morris team after lying at the mercy of the Western Approaches storms for 262 years.* (Daily Telegraph)

French cannon. It was not until the third bronze cannon was recovered that another piece of the jig-saw puzzle fitted together, for,
alongside the touch-hole, were roughly carved the letters that
spelled out V-I-G-O. Vigo was a Spanish Atlantic port and famous
in history for the Battle of Vigo Bay. There lay the clue as to why the
Association, an English man o'war, might be carrying a French cannon.

The amount of written documentation lying in the archives of
museums, libraries and various government offices around the
world is vast. The period covered is also immense; for example, in
the General Archives of the Indies in Seville, complete cargo mani-
fests still exist of voyages made back in the fifteenth century. There
is a record of the captain, crew, merchants and bankers of every
ship that ever voyaged to Spain's overseas possessions. The records
of a famous naval battle of 1702 are comparatively easy to locate
and it is possible to piece together the commander's various reports
to obtain a composite contemporary account of the complete action.
From Holland, from Spain, from London, documents recall the
Battle of Vigo Bay and the bounty and prizes seized by the Dutch
and English allies in 1702, from France and Spain. They link the
separate figures and careers of Sir George Rooke and Sir Cloudesley
Shovell and trace, too, the moment when Sir Cloudesley first caught
sight of the vessel he would make his own command, the stylish
Association of 96 guns—confirming the reason that *Association* became his treasure ship, for it was Vigo that provided Sir Cloudesley
with the bulk of his considerable fortune.

The story began a little before the battle when, during the war of
the Spanish succession, Marlborough was using the Royal Navy as a
strategic weapon to support the Army's campaign in Europe. The
Duke needed a Mediterranean base and an amphibious expedition
was staged against Cadiz. Admiral Sir George Rooke commanded an
enormous fleet of eighty men o'war with fifty transports carrying
ground troops commanded by the Duke of Ormonde, a man not
always in accord with Rooke. For much of the voyage Sir George was
sick and confined to his bed aboard *Somerset*. No doubt his lack of
physical fitness had much to do with the lamentable failure of this
enterprise. The troops landed and occupied the town but they indulged
in an orgy of drunkenness. Friction between land and sea commanders
resulted in little help from the Navy in establishing Cadiz as a base.
Consequently the troops re-embarked and Rooke set sail for

Sir George Rooke.
(Mansell Collection)

England, certain to be received in disgrace for his lack of endeavour. His whole future was in doubt, until he experienced a remarkable stroke of luck.

By September 21 the fleet was nearing Lisbon, when Rooke sent several ships in to Lagos Bay to water. One of the vessels was the sixty-gun *Pembroke*. Her captain was Thomas Hardy, a strong confident character who had amongst his officers a chaplain, Mr Beauvoir, a man of high intellect and resourcefulness. Beauvoir accompanied several officers ashore and there by accident met the French Consul, who, by all accounts, was a man much given to proclaiming the might of France. With a considerable amount of tact Beauvoir encouraged conversation and learned from this braggart that M. de Châteaurenault commanded a fleet—an invincible fleet, were the words used—that escorted twenty Spanish galleons loaded with specie and plate. This fleet lay at Vigo Bay.

Beauvoir returned to his ship and roused his captain from bed. Hardy in turn lost no time in crossing to the *Somerset* by small boat and insisted on waking his tetchy admiral in a manner that took no little courage. Rooke saw a chance to recover some lost glory and issued orders for the fleet to sail to Vigo, dispatching Hardy in the *Pembroke* to scout out the situation in Vigo Bay.

The regal sternboard from the Association *sold to Penzance for 'a load of potatoes.'* (Daily Telegraph)

Unknown to Rooke, English spies had already sent word to Queen Anne of a vast treasure fleet of twenty-one galleons loaded to the gunwales with a reputed thirty million pounds' worth of gold, silver and precious stones, commanded by Don Manuel de Velasco and escorted by twenty-three French men o'war. Because of European conflicts, the Plata Flotas had been delayed for two years and this fleet was one of the richest ever to cross the Atlantic. Such a treasure should not be allowed to reach Spain. The English Channel Fleet under Sir Cloudesley Shovell was dispatched to intercept. It had been the presence of Rooke at Cadiz and the knowledge that he was possibly sailing north that had forced de Châteaurenault, originally bound for Seville, to run for Vigo, there to prepare defences in case English Intelligence had gained knowledge of his fleet's whereabouts. His choice of Vigo was tactically sound, for its harbour of Redondela was capable of good defensive positions. What de Châteaurenault did not know was that the disgrace of Cadiz had transformed Rooke into a raging tiger. Nothing would stop him getting at the Spanish treasure galleons. Yet the French Admiral did prepare a formidable opposition.

During the afternoon of October 11, Rooke entered the Bay and anchored off Vigo. He was well aware of the precariousness of his position following the Cadiz debacle. If he waited for Sir Cloudesley Shovell, he would have to share the honours of Vigo with him— and Rooke's proportion of honours would not, perhaps, be enough to cancel out Cadiz. Rooke decided not to wait but to attack the next day. He called a council of war, with Ormonde and the Dutch Admiral Piet van der Goes. In the meantime he demanded intelligence of the French Commander's fortifications. An English lieutenant in a longboat investigated under cover of darkness and reported back that de Châteaurenault had prepared well. Across the narrow harbour mouth a boom of masts, cables, chains and casks was moored. At each end, a great man o'war was positioned; to port the seventy-gun *Espérance*, to starboard the sixty-eight gun *Bourbon*. Within the boom he had moored five other men o'war, bearing their broadsides on to the entrance. The remaining French fleet lay further up, out of range of English guns so long as the boom remained intact. Behind them, safe and secure, lay the Spanish treasure ships. No one had thought to remove the treasure chests inland.

A plan of action was detailed. The Duke of Ormonde would land with 2,500 troops to storm the south fort, while the mighty *Association* with *Barfleur* engaged the northside battery. As each engagement continued, a frontal attack by a combined English/Dutch fleet would crash the boom and attempt a break-through. The dubious honour of leading the boom attack eventually fell to Vice-Admiral Thomas Hopsonn in *Torbay* supported by Van der Goes in *Zeeven Provinciën*. Early in the morning of October 12 the attack began.

Rooke waited until Ormonde's ground troops attacked the south fortifications, taking all land works in a short, sharp engagement. He then ordered a frontal attack on the boom, while *Association* and *Barfleur* bombarded the north batteries. Formed up in line of battle, the van approached to within gunshot, when the wind died and the fleet was forced to re-anchor. After a few minutes' wait, a brisk breeze blew up. Thomas Hopsonn in *Torbay*, being nearest to the enemy, caused her cable to be cut and, making all sail, bore up to the boom under heavy fire from *Espérance* and *Bourbon*. *Torbay*, now moving rapidly, sails filling, banners streaming, her colours unfurled, hit the boom with a tremendous blow which caused it to give way. Hopsonn passed through and anchored inside, engaging both boom defence ships with resolute cannon fire. For a while, *Torbay* was in a vulnerable position but Van der Goes and other ships of *Torbay*'s division weighed their anchors and, hacking through the remnants of the boom defences, proceeded to assist their gallant colleague.

The Dutch flagship *Zeeven Provinciën* found the gap forced by *Torbay* and lay alongside *Bourbon*, quickly silencing and boarding the Frenchman, forcing her Captain to strike his colours. Vice-Admiral Hopsonn was particularly relieved to see *Bourbon* taken. His situation was still perilous but his gunners performed admirably under fire and broadside after broadside was poured into *Espérance*. The French hastily rigged a hulk as a fireship and sent it drifting down on *Torbay*, setting fire to the rigging. At that moment the laden hulk blew up alongside *Torbay*. The explosion proved providential for the hulk's cargo, tons of snuff, billowed up and then settled over *Torbay* putting out most of her fires. It was a situation that brought tears to Hopsonn's eyes and cleared the heads of both officers and men. *Torbay*, much damaged, was out of danger. *Association*'s mighty ironsides engaging the northern land-works, had silenced the guns from that quarter, without sustaining any damage herself, a fact that perhaps led to Sir Cloudesley later commandeering her for his own use; a fact, too, that led ultimately to the *Association*'s wrecking almost five years later in the Scilly Isles, loaded with 'Vigo' spoils and cannon.

De Châteaurenault was shaken by the swift turn of events. In little more than an hour his fortifications south and north were silenced, his boom cut to pieces, his defensive fireship gone. *Bourbon* was taken, *Espérance* destroyed and now the Allied fleet was bearing down upon him. Despairing of further defence he ordered his captains to fire their ships but, in the confusion, French and Spanish commanders were slow to follow de Châteaurenault's own action before the English and Dutch were upon them. A few ships were burnt but most were captured. Surviving officers and men fled ashore, although 400 were captured. Every enemy vessel, French and Spanish, was either captured or destroyed. It was a magnificent victory as the accounting would show. Rooke's honour was saved and he was not slow to record his gratitude.

Everyone in the fleet shared in the spoils, for the treasure and booty taken were of enormous value. Of the seventeen Spanish ships taken or burnt, five richly laden galleons became prizes of the Dutch and four of the English. The estimated value of gold and silver taken by the English came to thirteen million pieces-of-eight. Five French men o'war became prizes of the Royal Navy and were renamed.

Sir George Rooke was anxious to sail post-haste for England and acquaint his Sovereign and the Admiralty with a first-hand account of the Battle of Vigo Bay in the hope that it would erase the stigma of Cadiz. Normally the mopping up of prizes after such a victory would take up considerable time, time Rooke could ill afford now. His old friend and partner in many a commercial enterprise, Sir Cloudesley Shovell, was near at hand. He could entrust the culmination of the Vigo enterprise to him, knowing full well his own interests would be fully protected. Four days after the battle Sir Cloudesley brought his squadron into Vigo and was instructed by Sir George to refit the prizes, save as much treasure and as many guns as possible and complete the destruction of those vessels that could not be moved.

With Rooke on his way home, Sir Cloudesley was left in a most happy situation, for he shared a fine commercial instinct with Rooke. In the past, their trading around the Mediterranean, the bearing of bullion for bankers on commission—all quite above board for those times—had excited Samuel Pepys' displeasure during his period as Secretary to the Admiralty. Although such activities were common practice, Rooke and Shovell made a considerable career of it and Pepys was all for having them court-martialled until it was pointed out that both men also made a habit of winning fleet battles against the French and Spanish. Nonetheless both subsequently felt constrained to curb, to a slight extent, their merchant instincts.

Sir Cloudesley himself was no ordinary naval officer. At the time of Vigo Bay he was in his forties, a large-framed, portly figure of a man, a lover of the good things of life, although of humble origin. At nine years of age he had run away to sea from the miserable existence of an apprenticed boot cobbler. He became cabin boy to the first Admiral Byng and later to Admiral Narborough. A quick-

Two pairs of brass navigational dividers recovered from the wreck of Girona. *The lower pair, though bent, still works. The dividers are on a sixteenth-century navigational chart of the British Isles by Baptista Agnese.* (Ulster Museum)

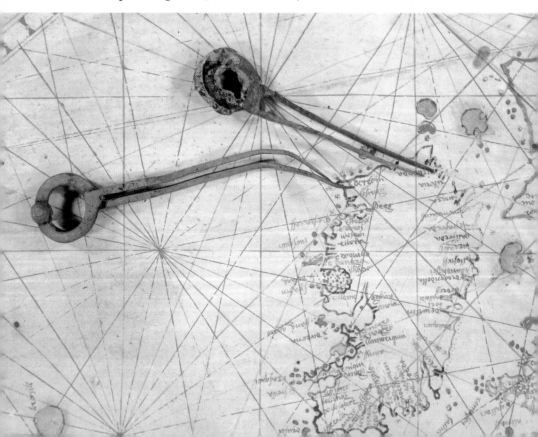

witted, courageous youth, he distinguished himself in action many times and rose from the lower decks to become an officer with the patronage of Admiral Narborough. Such a happening was rare and those few to achieve this status were known as 'Tarpaulins'. Sir Cloudesley's rise in rank was exceptionally successful and so were his merchant instincts.

At Vigo, therefore, he was delighted to busy himself among the treasure galleons and French men o'war, transferring giant bronze culverines into English ships, for the bore was the same. The letters V-I-G-O were stamped clearly on the cannon. Sir Cloudesley also greatly admired the ninety-six gun *Association* captained by William Bokenham, a good ship in a heavy sea, well built with spacious Admiral's quarters. He decided to transfer his flag and substantial chests of gold and silver coin—Escudos, Reis, Louis d'Or, Guineas, Reals, Crowns, Shillings—to the *Association*.

So the jig-saw pieces fitted together, by researching old records and reports—the French culverine, the Portuguese coin, the broad-arrow-mark cannon ball all had come together on board *Association* as a result of Vigo. But Roland Morris and his team were still unable to convince the authorities that the wreck below the Gilstones was indeed Sir Cloudesley's *Association*. After all, several years separated the action at Vigo Bay from the wreck of the *Association* off the Scillies in 1707. The Ministry of Defence, Her Majesty's Receiver of Wreck and marine archaeologists required more proof, which caused much heartache and more than a little trouble.

The search for underwater treasure always presents more problems than merely the locating of the wreck. Once the wreck has been discovered, who owns it? For example, the Netherlands Government, as successors to the giant VOC Dutch East India Company, own all its wreck. Written agreement is required to work and dispose of any retrieved items found on a Dutch East Indiaman, anywhere in the world. Authorities and governments everywhere have legal rights concerning wreck in their territorial waters. In United Kingdom waters, any item recovered from the sea must, by law, be notified to H.M. Receiver of Wreck, an officer usually found at the local Customs & Excise Office. A list of all finds should be supplied to that official within forty-eight hours of its discovery, where at all possible.

If ownership is not clear, the Receiver of Wreck is bound in law to advertise all finds made, by way of a droit list, retaining the

The Association. (Benbow/Morris Collection)

items (or, if too bulky, i.e. cannon, at an address of storage) for a period not less than one year and a day, after which a public auction is arranged for their disposal. Then, and only then, does the salvor gain his reward, a percentage awarded by the Board of Trade.

Until 1967, the United Kingdom had little, if any, experience of old sailing wreck treasure. An inadequate Act of Parliament, the Merchant Shipping Acts of 1894 and 1906, dictated the law, drafted in the main to cover items salvaged from fairly modern wrecks. If a wreck was a ship of the Royal Navy, ancient or modern, the Admiralty claimed ownership—now through the Ministry of Defence. Every item gathered from the sea—coin, plate, porcelain, ordnance, artifacts of every sort—already has an owner: the Crown, Admiralty, underwriters, Lords of the Manor, or a foreign Government. The diver, at best, can purchase the wreck. Alternatively, in a lowering order of preference, he can purchase sole salvage rights for an agreed sum; he can obtain sole diving rights for an agreed percentage from subsequent auctions; he can obtain sole diving rights, his return subject to an arbitrary award; or he can obtain non-exclusive diving rights relying on an ultimate reward. Such poorly defined, ambiguous 'rights' depended in the main on two things—wreck identification and the integrity of all divers. These were two outstanding problems that caused mayhem in UK waters in the early years of successful treasure finds.

In the United States a much simpler and more easily worked system prevails. The salvor is usually granted an exclusive contract, against a local State levy of twenty-five per cent of the total value of goods recovered, with a section of sea bed legally protected for the diver pending *later* identification of the wreck. In Spain a similar agreement is possible; the State requires between twenty and twenty-five per cent—shades of the old 'Royal Quinto' but very fair. The Netherlands Government operates parallel agreements with their percentage between twenty-five per cent and one-third, with the additional claim to purchase, at market value, any item the Dutch Government believes to be of particular historic value to the Netherlands. Other countries throughout the world vary their 'take' between twenty per cent and one-third, with historic 'rights to purchase' clauses in their agreements. In every case, a sectional sea bed location will be protected in law pending identification of wreck.

The United Kingdom was very different. In 1967 a non-exclusive diving agreement with the Ministry of Defence saw the Government taking between fifty per cent and two-thirds. The diver risked all for a miserable one-third, and then had to wait up to two years for the money. Such an attitude by the British Government stretched integrity to breaking point and later, when the rape of *Association* and other old wrecks began, it was hardly surprising that gold coins were being flogged for quick cash in bars all over Europe, in Brussels, Paris, Amsterdam, Antwerp, London.

A piece of history might change hands for ten pounds in any pub around England's West Country coast where, in the summer, tourists abound in their thousands—no questions asked. It was not until auctions began taking place at which coins that changed hands in pubs for ten pounds were sold for £350 and more that the 'trade' eased and more or less came to an end with increased rewards for divers in line with other countries. Of course, the 'trade' has not stopped completely, It never will. But there is less chance of 'losing history' than before. The main problem still remains, though—that of wreck identification.

Roland Morris's non-exclusive agreement with the Ministry of

Defence gave him the right '. . . to dive upon and carry out under-water salvage operations on four of Sir Cloudesley Shovell's squadron, namely the *Association, Eagle, Romney* and *Firebrand . . .*'

That agreement also authorized two other groups to dive beneath the Gilstones; Bob Rogers of the Lyonesse Salvage Company and the Sub Aqua Club of the Royal Naval Air Command, the original discoverers of a wrecksite at the Gilstone. But the agreement was useless until identification proved the wreck was *Association*. In the meantime every sub-aqua diver in England could dive on the wreck (and it seemed at times that they did!) quite legally, provided any item found was handed in to the Receiver of Wreck. It is open to considerable argument whether or not every item from *Association*'s wrecksite was handed in by those other than M.O.D. agreement holders. After all, it was not in the interests of non-agreement divers to help identify the wreck!

Throughout the summer of 1967, into early autumn, the Roland Morris team dived whenever possible, recovering a mass of items. Although Roland Morris himself was convinced that they were diving on the *Association*, the positive identification needed for the authorities continued to elude them. The first list of items recovered and notified to the Scillies Receiver of Wreck included six gold coins, 1,383 silver coins, three bronze cannon, one breech-loading bronze gun and dozens of historic artifacts. Such valuable finds could not be kept out of the newspapers nor off television screens. The headlines were large. In various countries newspapers ran many column inches, not always with a strict attention to the truth. Not surprisingly, perhaps, the *Scillonian*, a passenger/freighter that plies between Penzance on the English mainland and St Mary's, largest of the Scilly Isles, saw an increasing amount of Scuba gear and wild-eyed 'toughs' out for a little poaching.

With hindsight, it seems extraordinary that the authorities were not prepared to declare the wreck to be that of the *Association*. Specie that the Morris team brought up included English coins from the reigns of Charles II, James II, William and Mary and William III; Spanish coins of Philip II; French coins of Louis XIV— and not one coin was dated later than 1707, the year of the *Association*'s wreck!

Many of the coins had been recovered through the courage of Geoff Upton and Doug Rowe. As already described, the wrecksite beneath the Gilstone ledges is strewn with granite boulders over an area about the size of a soccer ground. Countless submarine caverns, caves and passages have been formed over a number of years by rock falls and subterranean storm currents. Consequently, searching the Gilstone is a hazardous business that has often to be undertaken in murky, dim conditions that make powerful torches a very necessary item of equipment. Late in September, Geoff and Doug were continuing a dive when Geoff spotted a cave formed by a pile of huge boulders. Shining his torch through the entrance, he saw that the hole opened up inside and looked well worth investigating, yet the opening was too narrow for him to get through with his air cylinder. Fifty feet below the surface, Geoff removed his back-pack and, still gripping his mouthpiece, carefully held his air cylinder before him and finned into the cave. The risk, in Geoff's opinion, was well worth it. The whole floor of the cave appeared to

Fatigue shows on the faces of divers Geoff Upton and Mark Horobin over the Association *wreck.* (Benbow/Morris Collection)

be lined with thousands of coins neatly arranged in rows. A fantastic discovery! But a discovery that would take weeks to work and the autumn was close upon them with the annual equinox gales.

Since only a couple of days of diving remained that year, the Morris team were left with the hope that their treasure cave would be there the following spring—a forlorn hope, as it turned out. For Roland Morris, 1967 had been a year of extraordinary ups and downs. He had certainly made some marvellous discoveries but he still had no positive identification of the wreck and the three official agreement holders had to watch as other divers tried their luck. It was imperative, in Roland Morris's view, to identify the wrecksite once and for all, before such a splendid historic site was ruined in the chase for gold. There was already evidence that dynamite was being used by some divers to split and shatter great boulders and iron cannon to get at the treasure below. Both Morris and fellow M.O.D. agreement holder Bob Rogers asked for help from the police and H.M. Receiver of Wreck to stop such action. The official answer was always the same: without positive identification that the site was that of the *Association* they were powerless to act.

Records exist in Britain in places such as the Public Records Office, the British Museum, the National Maritime Museum, Greenwich, and in City and Council Libraries, which throw considerable light on the life and times of notables long since dead and, in many cases, forgotten. From the town of Rochester in Kent, home town of Sir Cloudesley Shovell and the seat of his constituency as a Member of Parliament, a new insight into his life and marriage was obtained. A record of those officers who sailed with him on the *Association* was listed. In the Public Records Office there were reports of the scene of the 1707 shipwreck written by captains of ships who only by the barest of margins avoided a similar fate to that which overcame Sir Cloudesley and 2,000 of the men under his command. Gradually, their research took the Morris team from Vigo towards the point at which the *Association* ran against The Gilstone Rock.

Sir Cloudesley Shovell's career had blossomed after the Vigo Bay Battle and the subsequent sharing out of prize money. On the death of his former patron, Admiral Sir John Narborough, Sir Cloudesley married the widow and, in turn, looked after the old admiral's children. The Narborough heir, also Sir John, accompanied Sir Cloudesley on the *Association*, as did his younger brother, James, as well as Henry, the son of Bishop Trelawney of Winchester. Captain Edmund Loades was Flag Captain aboard the *Association* and Captain Whitaker her Sailing Master. One midshipman was Thomas Pitt, a member of the family from whom the Earls of Chatham would rise.

In 1706, Sir Cloudesley had been promoted Admiral of the Blue and Commander in Chief of the Mediterranean Fleet. A year later, Admiralty orders called for Sir Cloudesley to leave thirteen ships at Gibraltar under Sir Thomas Dilkes, for winter service in the Mediterranean, and to proceed home with the rest of his fleet. Accordingly, Sir Cloudesley set sail in his beloved *Association*, leading a fleet of fifteen ships-of-the-line, five frigates and a fast yacht. With Sir George Byng, Vice-Admiral of the Blue, flying his flag in the *Royal Anne*, and Sir John Norris, Rear-Admiral of the Blue, in *Torbay* of Vigo fame, it was a formidable fleet, well officered.

Sir Cloudesley was in haste to get home and the weather did its part in pushing the fleet along. Indeed, passage up the Portuguese and Spanish coast and through Biscay was beset by equinox gales which rolled up massive seas astern and formed a low cloud base with sheety rain that followed day after day. Navigational instruments were still primitive, compasses were unreliable and, when shooting a sun-sighting for latitude, crude backstaffs were far from satisfactory. As for longitude, the chronometer had only been invented by Harrison in 1671 and was not yet in common use on the sea. Without a sun-sighting, buffeted by winds and high seas, Sir Cloudesley, his Flag Captain and Sailing Master were unsure of their position. On the afternoon of October 21, signal flags were flown to order soundings to be taken and the fleet to hove-to while Sailing Masters joined the *Association* for a navigational conference.

When nearing shallow waters great value was placed upon soundings, not just for depth of water but for evidence of the sea bed. Thus leadsmen would swing hollow, lead-weighted lines, the lead being packed with tallow wax. Particles of the sea bed would adhere to the wax. Charts of those times not only had depths marked but sea bed traces also.

Sir Cloudesley declared that the way for the English Channel lay directly ahead and ordered the fleet to follow his stern lantern home.

The wreck of the Eagle. (Benbow/Morris Collection)

Within hours the fleet found itself amongst the rocks and inlets that lie to the south-west of the Scillies. Desperately manoeuvring to avoid destruction, the seventy-gun *Eagle* drove onto the Crim Rocks and sank with the loss of all hands, 440 men. With that turbulent sea she was smashed to pieces within minutes. The *Romney*, of fifty guns, ran into Tearing Ledge—there were no survivors from her complement of 280 men. Between Black Rock of Annet and Carnew Rock of St Agnes, *Firebrand* struck a reef and sank. Fortunately, Captain Piercy led twenty-two of his crew of forty-five to safety.

Finally, the flagship herself, the mighty *Association*, ran onto the Gilstone Ledges, stuck fast and began to break up. What happened on board can only be conjecture. In fact, the Admiral's barge was got away and with it a chest or two of coin, the Admiral, the two Narborough boys, Henry Trelawney and two other persons. But not one of the 680 men who had been aboard survived. Sir Cloudesley's capsized barge made it to shore, driven some distance from the Outer Gilstone, and grounded at Porth Hellick, a cove on St Mary's Island. At daybreak the Admiral's body, with those of his companions, was found and buried above high water mark. His *Association*, loaded with a vast treasure reputed to be valued at £3,000,000, lay seventy feet deep below the Gilstone.

76

An account such as this, of the last hours of Sir Cloudesley's fleet, can be pieced together by anyone who spares the time to read through information buried deep in Naval documents and old journals. Some treasure hunters might believe that hours spent in research on dry land would be better spent in research on the sea bed but time after time the indisputable identity of a wreck has come as the result of knowledge gained by hours of study. The *Association* was to prove this once again.

The Morris team continued to bring up quantities of coin and pieces of jewellery from the wreck. Among these items were posy rings (from the French '*poésie*')—gold rings with lovers' inscriptions, popular amongst sailors for many, many years. Simple expressions of love wound round the inside of such rings: 'God Above Increase our Love' read one; 'Not the Value But My Love' another; 'True Love is Endless' yet a third; 'In thy Sight is my Delight' a fourth; and an English version of the ring that Robert Sténuit had found from the *Girona*. This time it read, in English: 'I have Nothing More to give Thee'. The two rings indicated a span of more than a hundred years of sea tradition.

Already the very first discoveries brought to the surface in 1967, the year before, were being prepared for auction by the Scillies Receiver of Wreck, the statutory year and a day having long gone by. And yet, despite overwhelming circumstantial evidence, the *Association* still remained stubbornly unidentified, at least to the authorities. Two particular items very nearly tipped the balance of evidence. One was a late seventeenth century silver *étui*/toothpick case three-and-a-half inches high, the base being engraved with a coat of arms identified as those of the Pitt family—Thomas Pitt, the midshipman known to have been aboard the *Association*. Another was that of a silver dog-nose spoon with rat-tail bowl and flat stem, the back of the terminal engraved with a crest of an upright mailed fist and similar to a crest used by both Captain Edmund Loades, Flag Captain of the *Association*, and her Sailing Master, Captain Whitaker. In the eyes of authority, however, even these items were 'Not proof enough'.

Meanwhile all and sundry made more than a meal out of the *Association*, ravaging the wrecksite indiscriminately. Roland Morris was enraged at the despoliation of such a haven of British nautical history. He enlisted the help of his local Member of Parliament,

John Nott, and began the fight to frame a new law to protect historic wrecks in British waters. But at last came the kind of proof that even the reluctant authorities had to accept.

A new diver to the Morris team, Mark Horobin, made the discovery; it would not have been surprising if he had missed it. He found a silver plate, almost folded in half and covered in a hard sea-growth; the silver was oxidised black. When the calcinous growths were carefully—most carefully—removed and the blackened silver cleaned and straightened, there was revealed a magnificent silver dinner plate with a crest clear and undamaged—the crest of Sir Cloudesley Shovell. The right hand side contained the arms of the Narborough family, the left side shewed honours, in chief two crescents Argent (a victory over Turkish Forces), in base a Fleur de Lis Or (for success against the French). These honours were awarded to Sir Cloudesley by Letters Patent in January 1692. The proof was at last indisputable but it was almost too late for the poor *Association*. Her site had been thoroughly pillaged; it was a sad situation. Thousands of coins, plate, jewellery and heaven-only-knew-what valuable historic artifacts had by-passed H.M. Receiver of Wreck or had simply been destroyed.

As an immediate result of the proof, civil law rights could be applied to protect those Ministry of Defence licence holders—but would that protection work in practice? The rights of 'Salvor in Possession' required that a buoy be placed over the site. Any poachers found diving could then be brought to court by the licence holders in a civil action. But the Gilstone site is so remote that to moor such a buoy was an open invitation to the scavengers—it was just impossible to monitor the site twenty-four hours a day. Coins still found their way onto the continent in spite of Interpol investigations. There was, however, one good result of the legal identification. An auction, the very first of its kind in Britain, could be advertised officially as a sale of items from the *Association*. Sotheby's New Bond Street salerooms held the historic sale in July 1969, a sale of artifacts from a wreck of 1707 by a firm which, as Baker, Leigh and Sotheby, was established only thirty-seven years after the wreck.

English milled gold guineas and half-guineas; Brazilian gold reis; French Louis d'Or; English silver crowns; half-crowns, shillings and sixpences; Brazilian, Mexican and Peruvian minted Spanish reales of eight; historic silver and plate; gold and silver jewellery; French bronze cannon—all came under the hammer. It was a memorable day. Altogether 136 lots, comprising 2,359 items, were sold.

An auction gallery can be an exciting market place and so it was that hot July day with the mahogany panelled gallery packed with numismatists and collectors of historic silver and jewellery. The auction attracted the national newspapers and a number of their representatives were also in attendance.

At 11 a.m. precisely on Monday, July 14, 1969, the sale began: 'Lot number one. A Charles Second English guinea milled gold piece of 1668, third bust, pointed truncation, plain below, obverse damaged to last "A" in Gratia but otherwise fair— what am I bid?'

Every coin tells a detailed story to the expert, whether the profile of King or Queen depicts a full wig or half, or where the progress of a reign can be traced by differing busts as the monarch matures in years: a first bust, a second, a third; whether the King's brow is exposed or not, whether the coin was minted and hand hammered or machine milled. A single letter would denote whether it came from new branch mints York, Chester, Norwich or Exeter. A rose between the coats of arms would indicate silver from West Country mines. Special silver would indicate its source, as with the 'Vigo' stamp. The condition of coins offered for sale follows an agreed and accepted code: therefore, in order of perfection, coins are listed as proof, mint state, extremely fine, very fine, good.

Foreign gold and silver coins have an equally interesting history. The famed silver mints of Lima, Potosi and Mexico City produced coins by the million, pieces-of-eight, a form of currency known the world over. While quality of silver refining at times caused problems—at least one Ensayador at Potosi was put to death, in 1649, for 'default in keeping the legal weight and fineness of minted coin' —such was their confidence in the piece-of-eight that Spanish, Portuguese, Dutch and English traders all used it. European traders reported the popularity of the coin with Chinese merchants in the saying 'Plata sa sangue'—'Silver is their life's blood'.

The first foreign gold coin to be sold was that recovered from the *Association* by Doug Rowe. It came under the hammer as Lot 72, its historic value further enhanced because it had been the very first recovered coin of all: 'Lot 72. A gold 4,000 reis from the Rio mint in Brazil; a Peter the Second coin dated 1703, edge is slightly damaged, obverse has slight corrosion and creasing but otherwise about "very fine" and "rare". Shall we start at fifty pounds?' A catalogue was raised. 'Thank you, at fifty pounds then—sixty—seventy-five—thank you', the auctioneer expertly scanned the room, already he knew the most likely buyers. 'Seventy-five then, and eighty—and ninety, one hundred, yes, one hundred—and ten—and twenty, thank you. At one hundred-and-twenty pounds', he glanced at the back of the hall, 'Against you', he paused—'At one hundred-and-twenty!', he rapped his rostrum with an ebony hammer and murmured a name to his clerk.

Next came a Louis XIV d'Or about 'fine and scarce' which was sold for £150. So the sale progressed. Some lots of badly corroded coin were lumped together. One such lot comprised 42 coins with a gross silver weight of about 10 ounces.

There were coins and dates that caused numismatists to pay new record prices. 'Lot 85. A most interesting coin, a gold Portuguese 4,000 reis of John the Fifth, 1707, the first year of a new reign, slight creasing but otherwise almost "extremely fine and rare". The only

Recovered from the Association—*a unique, beautifully embellished bronze 'Honour' cannon, cast by Thomas Pit in 1604 and commissioned by the Earl of Devonshire, Master of Ordnance in that year. The cannon honoured the Prince of Wales.* (F. E. Gibson)

coin English or foreign dated 1707, the year of the wreck, to come from *Association*. A marvellous piece of history. At . . . seventy-five pounds I am bid . . . eighty-five . . . one hundred . . .' So bid quickly followed bid.

Prices were higher than expected. Perhaps it was the romance of an old wreck. At last, the coin, the jewellery, the posy rings, the artifacts, were all gone. All that remained were lot numbers 135 and 136, the two French culverine cannon. They were bronze giants of three tons with a barrel length of 115 inches and a bore diameter of five and three-quarter inches. Lot 135, a Louis XIII cannon, was embellished with *fleurs de lys* alternating with leaves and acanthus foliage, the breech cast with the arms of France, adorned with those of Navarre within collars of the Orders of St Michael and St Esprit; above the vent, crossed anchors and chased dolphins and forward a crowned monogram of Louis XIII; a foresight in the form of a salamander. The date on the breech moulding was 1638. It was a magnificent piece.

Bidding began cautiously, this was new ground for those interested and three tons of metal is not a practical acquisition for everyone. But the bidding increased until the cannon was knocked down at £3,000 to gunsmiths Holland and Holland. The second cannon, the last lot in the sale, was embellished in much the same manner as the first but cast to an august personality, le Comte de Vermandois, a title of singular note in French chivalry, bestowed upon an illegitimate son of Louise de la Vallière, a mistress of Louis XIV. In 1669, as a two-year old, the baby was created Lord High Admiral of France. Alas, the boy died when only sixteen without leaving an heir and the Vermandois title died with him, never to be used again. This cannon too was sold for £3,000; again the purchaser was Holland and Holland.

The sale realized just short of £20,000; the Ministry of Defence recovered fifty per cent of the proceeds of coin, plate and jewellery. From the cannons, Roland Morris received the full price, less sale expenses. The first sale in Britain ever devoted entirely to sunken treasure concluded with an awakened interest by collectors in the acquisition of wreck items. The auctions that followed realized successively higher totals—£50,000, then £100,000—as more wrecks were discovered and more coin and plate, much of it in mint condition, was put up for sale.

6

Robert Sténuit and the Witte Leeuw

There were many others besides Roland Morris spending winter hours researching old documents in the attempt to produce adequate proof of identification. During the winter of 1967, Robert Sténuit was desperately searching for clues to prove the identity of 'his' wreck in Northern Ireland as the Armada galleass *Girona*.

English law was clear on the point of established precedent, that any salvor who is working uninterruptedly on a wreck he has discovered *and buoyed* becomes known as 'salvor in possession' and can protect his rights in a civil court of law against any trespassers. Clearly enough, the onus was on Sténuit to protect himself. But he and Marc Jasinski had used the summer of 1967 as the time for an exploratory survey. Having found what they truly believed to be the *Girona* they would have to leave for the winter and return in the spring of 1968 with a team of divers to work the wreck and map and chart all finds for a full archaeological report. What would happen if someone else stumbled on the wreck in the meantime?

Sténuit was concerned with the problem but could do little about it. A new law to protect historic wrecks was needed on the United Kingdom statute book but, as the law stood, Sténuit was required to inform the local Receiver of Wreck at Coleraine of his discoveries and, for the rest, hope that the news would not leak out and bring those poaching divers too lazy to find their own wreck sites. Sténuit and Jasinski left Ireland and returned to their businesses, vowing to research that winter to fill in, where at all possible, gaps of information about the *Girona* and who sailed with her at the time of her wrecking.

By the spring of 1968 Robert Sténuit was back in Portballintrae, diving below the Chimney Tops, this time with a team of eight divers and equipment kindly loaned by Henri Delauze. Fearing that their site would have been discovered by someone else, it was with some trepidation that Robert and Marc dived again. Much to their relief, it had been left alone and they decided to start the season by a lift of one of the cannon. Sketches of the new sea bed were made and grid charts drawn—although, with that current-race, such charts were of valid accuracy only on one tide. Marine archaeology in Northern European waters bears no relation to that carried out in the relatively placid Mediterranean.

The cannon was a breech-loading bronze Esmeril, around five feet long and weighing about a ton. A lifting bag was attached and an air cylinder opened beneath. As air expanded the bag in a mass of tiny silver bubbles, the cannon slowly began to move upwards. Luckily, in a depth of twenty feet or so, there is very little expansion of air at reduced water pressure and Sténuit's team were able to complete the lift without difficulty. It was much easier work than the time in the Scillies, when a Naval Air Command Sub-Aqua Club lifted a bronze cannon by similar means but in a greater depth of water. The expansion of air was then such that the lift became uncontrollable; the huge bronze cannon raced faster and faster to the surface, bursting through and leaping a few feet into the air. No one was injured, but it was a close call for those topsides in a rubber dinghy.

Drawings were made and photographs taken of items revealed by the removal of the cannon, which included a sounding lead. Then, still attached to its lifting bag, the cannon was towed behind one of the Zodiac inflatables back to Portballintrae. The courteous people of that area had always left the divers well alone but the recovery of an old cannon was not something that occurred every day. Within hours, minutes it seemed, the news was out. Newspapers in Ireland and England contained various accounts of the cannon and possible Armada wreck discovery. Reporters gathered in the local pubs, quickly reinforced by a television crew. Their questions were predictable: Was there a wreck? Was it from the Armada? How old is the cannon? Have you found any gold? Who owns the wreck? Sténuit's answers did not really satisfy anyone but until he had positive identification there was little he could say with any certainty.

Twelve divers from Belfast arrived at Portballintrae the following Sunday, studiously avoiding the Sténuit team as they loaded a hired local boat with their diving gear, small pick-axes, tyre levers, sacks and lifting balloons. Sténuit introduced himself and tried to talk to them in vain.

There was no response. Sténuit advised the boat-owner of his own legal position but again seemed to make little impression on anyone. Determined not to be forced off the site, Sténuit and members of his team boarded the *Zodiac* and headed for Lacada Point.

With members of the team above the water in the boat and others below the surface, they watched as the poachers divided into teams and proceeded to dive, using the buoy ropes and guide lines of Robert Sténuit's own divers. One particular line led in to a part of the wrecksite of which Sténuit maintained high hopes and there to greet the pirates was a large and forbidding member of Sténuit's team. Quickly the Irish divers wheeled away. Another team, using guide lines, examined breech blocks and then moved further out to sea. Sténuit himself saw yet a third team working around the sea bed and dived to check them closer, just in time to see a diver pick up a lump of lead and place it in his bag.

Sténuit finned down to him, touched him on the shoulder and shook his head at the man. He emptied the diver's bag and let the lead fall to the bed in its original position. Immediately Sténuit was surrounded by angry gesticulating divers. One held his air cylinder while another grabbed his fins. Furious, Sténuit pushed and tried to kick his assailants off. He made for the surface, where more Irish divers moved towards him. At that moment the Belgian's second *Zodiac* buzzed around Lacada Point with the rest of Sténuit's team. The two groups faced each other, angry men in a dangerous environment, black hoods bobbing in the Atlantic swell. Fortunately one of the Irish reminded the others that they were a club and, swearing dire reprisals against the 'foreigners', they departed, leaving the Sténuit team angry and bewildered, for at all times they had acted

Lacada Point, near Portballantrae, Co. Antrim—'the cruel talon of rock', as Robert Sténuit described it. The galleass Girona *struck on the seaward end.* (Ulster Museum)

strictly within the letter of the law. Since they were already at the site Sténuit told his team to relieve their tensions in a little work.

When, later, they arrived back at Portballintrae, Sténuit found a large policeman waiting. Apparently one of the poachers had complained of violence, although he could not substantiate his charge. Sténuit found the police polite and a little embarrassed.

London daily newspapers had a field day with their headlines: 'Spanish Treasure Ship Divers in Under Sea Clash' (*Daily Mirror*)' 'Storm on the Sea Bed as Rival Divers Clash' (*Daily Mail*), 'Deep Sea Fight over Wreck' (*Daily Express*). Further reports came from the BBC and Radio Belfast.

But on May 31, 1968, Mr Justice Lowry of the Supreme Court of Judicature in Northern Ireland, proclaimed: 'There is good evidence that Mr Sténuit is indeed the exclusive salvor in possession . . .' At last there could be no dispute and no further fears of trespassing. The remaining hours in a short diving season were devoted to fully charting the site and combing the wreck over for cast-iron evidence that this was the *Girona*.

Once the whole area had been charted and photographed, a trigonometrical plan was drawn up on which the exact position of every object was marked before any retrieval was made. When all this had been accomplished, the team were free to bring up to the surface anything they could find, a task that would involve more than one season. It was a slow, painstaking job conducted in bitterly cold water, hazy visibility, strong currents and kelp weed. Nonetheless, during the period worked, Robert Sténuit and his divers returned to the light of day more than 3,000 items.

There was a total of 405 gold coins that ranged from Joan the Mad through Charles V, John III and Philip II, including a rare Neapolitan gold ducat. There were marvellous gold jewels, one a beautifully made golden salamander which at one time contained a row of rubies along its back. There were eleven sixteenth century Italian cameos of lapis lazuli bearing the profile of Roman Emperors within an enamelled setting of gold and pearls. There were a dozen gold rings and eight gold chains, one nearly eight feet long and four pounds in weight. Such chains had been an instant form of ready money, for they were worn around the neck by noblemen, who would remove a link or two as necessary to settle an account. There are portraits in which sixteenth century noblemen can be seen wearing these chains of currency.

More than 700 silver coins were recovered as well as 115 made of copper. Nautical instruments included two astrolabes, five dividers, three sounding leads and a couple of hour-glasses. There were two bronze cannon, a musket and fragments of flint lock pistols. A number of swords and dagger handles were recovered. Silver dishes; lead ingots and weights; pewter tankards, pots, bowls and dishes; bronze buckles, powder pestles and mortars, nails and pins; copper cooking pots, hooks and handles; glass bottles; pottery vases; leather objects—a whole array of sixteenth century Spanish history. In monetary terms the total value was in excess of £30,000 but in terms of marine archaeology the prize was simply priceless.

There was one particular object that gave great personal delight to Robert Sténuit. Piece by piece a gold cross of a Knight of Malta was recovered and assembled. From a motif carved in the angles of the cross, Stenuit proved the *Girona* wreck, for the motif was known to feature in the Spinola family coat of arms. The Malta Cross had belonged to the captain of *Girona*, Don Fabricio Spinola. There was no longer any doubt of the identity of the 1588 galleass.

Sténuit's love of hunting the sea bed for long lost treasures heightened his thirst for historical knowledge and the desire to share that knowledge with others. After a number of years of delicate negotiation, he donated many of the items he had recovered to the Ulster Museum of the Northern Ireland National Museum and there, on June 22, 1972, the collection was opened in the 'Girona Rooms'. It was a generous and very fitting action by Europe's outstanding treasure hunter.

Meanwhile, Sténuit was compiling an extensive list from among the wrecks that abounded throughout the world, of those that might be worth his attention. Would it be a possible Dutch VOC wreck, the *Witte Leeuw* off St Helena? Or the British 66-gun man o'war, *Athénienne*, off Sicily? Or the *Sprightly*, near Guernsey? Or would he go back to Vigo after a Spanish galleon? The winter was the time for the research that would determine his next quarry.

It was to Sicily that he turned first. The 66-gun British *Athénienne* was wrecked off the Esquierquiers Reef on October 20, 1806. In command was Captain Rainsford. The subsequent court martial held on the *Royal George* under the presidency of Vice-Admiral Sir Thomas Duckworth, found that the *Athénienne* could have been influenced by current but, in any case, the course steered was too near for safety, particularly at night. However, the surviving officers were acquitted of all blame. Altogether 347 lives were lost and a cargo of 40,000 pieces-of-eight plus the ship's English coin ended up below the treacherous reefs.

Robert Sténuit set up an expedition to search for *Athénienne* and, accompanied by Marc Jasinski and other divers, spent five months searching the reefs. Careful research and painstaking work eventually brought them reward. Besides cannon and ballast, enough artifacts were discovered to confirm identification of the wreck. Of the known 40,000 pieces-of-eight only 4,000 were in fact recovered and of these 3,500 had been badly scoured by sea bed action. The rest, however, protected where they had fallen down deep crevices, were undamaged. These included pillar dollar eight-reales from the

Gold Cross of a Knight of the Order of Malta, originally covered with white enamel, traces of which still survive. The fleur-de-lys motifs between the arms of the cross suggest that it belonged to the Genoese Fabricio Spinola, captain of the Girona. (Ulster Museum)

mints of Seville, Madrid, Santiago and New Guatemala.

'Pillar' dollars are so called because they depict the Pillars of Hercules flanking the hemisphere on their obverse. The encircling script reads 'Plus Ultra'—'more beyond'—indicating the continuing scope and breadth of the Spanish Empire. A machine for this form of coin was first introduced into Mexico City in 1732, a date which has become greatly significant to numismatists, as coin auctions prove.

Among the bulk of the coins recovered, there were more pillar dollars—from Lima, Potosi, Guatemala, Santiago, Mexico and from

the mints of Metropolitan Spain at Madrid and Seville. These included coins from the reigns of Charles III and Charles IV and coins
that would later form part of a unique auction of coin and artifacts
from nine wrecks.

It was the lonely island of St Helena that next captured Sténuit's
attention—a pinprick in the vast wastes of the South Atlantic. To
the North, by slightly West, Ascension Island appears as another
pinprick, almost 1,000 miles distant; to the South, the dot of
Tristan de Cunha is more than 1,200 miles away; to the East, the
nearest mainland, South West Africa, is almost as far; to the West,
lies Brazil, nearly 2,000 miles from St Helena. This small volcanic
island, only 55 square kilometres in area, made a most suitable
prison for Napoleon from 1815 to 1821. But its value to Sténuit lay
in its position along the line of the trade winds. With its soaring
mountain peaks, there are plenty of rain-water springs, with
crystal-clear water, and in days gone by St Helena proved to be a
convenient staging post for ships homeward bound for Europe from
India and the Far East. The carracks and naus or fast freighters, of
Portuguese, Dutch and English traders put in for fresh water and
fresh meat, for there were plenty of wild pigs as well.

For weeks on end Sténuit pored over the reports of masters of
vessels sailing to and fro between mainland Europe and the treasure
sources of India, the Spice Islands and China. In the early 1600s, a
state of war had existed between the Seven United Provinces of
Holland and Portugal over rights to the Spice Islands. Holland had
raided various Portuguese settlements and built in turn their own
fortresses in Malacca, Batavia, Sumatra and Bantam, evicting the
Portuguese wherever they were found, in fierce and bloody battles.
By 1610 the Dutch East India Company had virtual domain over
the Spice Islands and ruled with a heavy, autocratic hand.

At sea the Portuguese and Dutch fought regularly and vessels of
both nationalities were accustomed to sail in convoy for mutual
protection. Masters' reports spoke of many battles and evasive
actions. Convoys unhesitatingly attacked numerically inferior
forces and such was the enmity between the two sides that prisoners
were never taken, even for ransom.

With rapid expansion of the Dutch VOC, and an increasing
number of ships with which they were able to ply the Far East
trade, St Helena became a dangerous place for the Portuguese.

Instructions were issued to masters of returning carracks to avoid making traditional water and provision stages there. But it appears that instructions were ignored in 1613 by Capitao Jeronimo d'Almeido when master of the armed nau *Casa da Nossa Senhora da Nazare* and accompanied by the nau *Conceicao*.

D'Almeido's report confirmed that, due to lack of fresh water and food, his two naus had anchored to replenish supplies. It was unfortunate for him that five Dutch East Indiamen then sailed into the bay and, perceiving the Portuguese vessels apparently helpless at anchor, streamed their battle banners and attacked, confident in their superior numbers and mobility. They met with a surprise. Since the Armada of 1588, Portuguese gunners had been trained by Germans and Italians, who were acknowledged throughout Europe as the finest in their skill. The *Nazare*'s gunners were both experienced and proficient.

As the Dutch squadron manoeuvred into a line-ahead formation, with the *Witte Leeuw*—'White Lion'—in the van, d'Almeido, judging wind and tide, calculated the Dutchman's path and warped the *Nazare* into a broadside position to receive the Dutch attack. The *Witte Leeuw* sailed into a cannonade of blisteringly accurate fire. Before she was able to withdraw from the confines of the bay, she was raked again and holed many times on the waterline. A second Dutch ship also received devastating damage and the whole Dutch squadron hurriedly withdrew, to lick their wounds. Those of the *Witte Leeuw* were fatal. She was sinking rapidly. A few of her crew were taken on board other vessels but there was no saving the ship. *Witte Leeuw* sank at the entrance to the bay she had so fearlessly entered. It was a disaster for the masters of the VOC vessels who most certainly returned home to the blistering criticism of the directors of the VOC, the Heeren XVII.

The Portuguese had, in fact, achieved a remarkable feat of arms, for it was a considerable reversal of fortune for an anchored Portuguese nau to inflict such damage in so short a time: the reloading of cannon was a time-consuming business that often involved up to ten minutes between volleys. The answer to the Portuguese success may have been in an old trick of Drake's. Once, at anchor, bombarding a Spanish town and fortress, Drake's master gunner, an old Dartmouth man, loaded both port and starboard guns. Having fired one broadside, he ran the port guns back to reload, replacing them with the starboard guns, and thereby halving the time between salvos.

The *Witte Leeuw* had been an Amsterdam Chamber vessel and the records show that on January 30, 1610 she left Amsterdam in convoy with seven other vessels under the command of Governor-General Pieter Both. For two years she traded around the Moluccas and the Celebes; her captain was Roelof Symoensen de Blom. In 1613, with three other Dutch VOC ships, *Witte Leeuw* sailed home to Europe from Bantam. In a letter written from the Amsterdam VOC to the Governor-General in Bantam, there appeared the passage:

'. . . The loss of the ship *Witte Leeuw*, near St Helena, when attacking two Portuguese carracks which had there come at anchor . . . are mighty heavy blows for the company. . . . '

Witte Leeuw had been a vessel of 150 feet length and 25 feet beam; she carried the usual fore, main and mizzen masts; her burthen was about 750 tons and she sailed with a complement of 200 including crew, VOC soldiers and passengers. From two years trading around the Spice Islands, she would have been heavy laden with the goods and produce of that exotic region. But, since she was homeward bound, she would probably not be carrying coin or bullion. And there were those who doubted whether, after 360 years beneath the sea, there would be anything left at all either of the vessel or its cargo. Robert Sténuit thought otherwise. He felt that his team would have a reasonable chance of finding the wreck despite the passage of time since her loss.

The site referred to in VOC records as Kerk Baaij was modern Jamestown Bay, the capital and harbour of the island. In 1976 Sténuit, his company of four divers and archaeologists, known as 'Groupe de Rechérche Archaeologique Sous-Marine Post Médiévale' began diving into Jamestown Bay, quartering a search pattern, section by section. The sea was cold at depth but clear until one encountered the bottom where hundreds of years of alluvial deposits, washed into the bay by heavy rains flooding down from the high peaks, had built up a sticky silt of mud many feet thick. Sténuit found the *Witte Leeuw* at a depth of a hundred feet buried under nine feet of slimy, cloudy mud!

Two massive nine-foot-long bronze cannon of the Amsterdam Chamber of the VOC served to identify the *Witte Leeuw*. As usual with such long-lost wrecks, little remained of her structure, although

One hundred and fifty years after battle, a French naval cannon comes to the surface. (Dave Burrell)

Sténuit had hoped that, because of the thickness of mud, more of her timbers might have been preserved than with other wrecks. Alas, it was not so. The wreckage was widely scattered and only a small section of the bottom hull was recognisably part of a ship. When touched, that wood, become a messy pulp, broke up and streamed away with the current like black smoke.

Sténuit and his team mapped, recorded, surveyed and excavated the site for seven months. Many artifacts were recovered, items of wood, leather, pewter, silver and glass. They even discovered pieces of porcelain, shattered into small fragments in the wreck and by the passage of time. And then, to their astonishment, deep in the mud, near the section of the bottom hull, they found part of the *Witte Leeuw*'s cargo of pepper, from which they extracted dozens of intact and perfect items of Chinese porcelain of the Ming Emperor period Wan Li! These magnificent examples of old Chinese art had been protected by the peppercorn for 360 years on the Southern Atlantic Ocean seabed. Sténuit had achieved another marvellous find.

There were Kraak porcelain dishes, winecups, tazzas; teabowls; winepots and covers; covered and open bowls; kendi; Swatow bowls; whole sets of plates and dishes, winecups and kendi with beautifully coloured paintings and decorations of birds and flowering plants, water scenes and Buddhist motifs; gloriously patterned plates and bowls—an almost unbelievable treasure hoard of centuries-old Chinese art was recovered from the sea.

In part, the clue to the miracle lay in the common practice amongst colonial Dutch returning home to Holland from service in Indonesia, who packed their precious glass, jade and porcelain in coffee beans for protection. Peppercorns proved a satisfactory alternative, a sensible safeguard, practised as long as old Dutch colonials can remember.

Back in France, Robert Sténuit began to catalogue his finds. Auctions were arranged both in Amsterdam, where Sotheby Mak van Waay B V sold cannon and porcelain, and at Sotheby's in London, where 49 lots of porcelain from the Ming dynasty of

A diver returns to the surface with a hoard of coins within a mass of sea growth. (Dave Burrell)

Chinese porcelain of the last Ming Emperor, Wan Li, recovered by Sténuit from the Dutch East-Indiaman Witte Leeuw. *Originally packed in a bulk pepper cargo, hundreds of pieces were found still intact and perfect after 360 years beneath the sea. Lot 68 is on the left.* (Sotheby Parke Bernet & Co.)

Emperor Wan Li came up for sale on March 15, 1977. This division of treasure revealed another side to the business. In the United Kingdom, where the Receiver of Wreck is responsible for arranging auctions through his administrative department, that of Trade and Industry, the early days taught many lessons about marketing treasure to obtain the best possible price. As auctioneers and companies of fine art dealers had experienced, specialized sales brought the best returns. A general auction of wreck items which included coins, silver artifacts, porcelain, gold ornaments and jewellery proved unlikely to realize the sort of prices that were possible when

94

the treasure was split up into several auctions: coins for the numismatists; silver and pewter plate; porcelain; nautical artifacts. Despite the proven success of this method, the Department of Trade
and Industry still tend to lump their sales together.

It was easier for Sténuit to arrange 'his' auction because of the
flexibility in law, the *Witte Leeuw* being of Dutch origin.

In a specialized auction of Chinese ceramics and works of art
there were 49 lots of *Witte Leeuw* porcelain. It was significant, in a
sale that comprised 184 lots, that the wreck items realized the best
prices and even Sotheby's were surprised at how much they did
realize, although items from wrecks had been consistently reaching
figures much higher than the normal market rate and, of course, the
history of the porcelain from the *Witte Leeuw* was unique. The first
Witte Leeuw sale was of two kraak porcelain dishes, each decorated
in underglaze-blue with a central shaped panel, one depicting a
galloping pony, the other a waterbird beside a lake, each reserved
on different diaper grounds and encircled around the cavetts with
medallions of precious objects alternating with peach and flower
sprigs below the barbed everted rim. Each dish stood about eight
inches high. They were predominantly blue and white, the drawings
light and full of craftsmanship.

Bidding was very brisk and the first item of *Witte Leeuw* treasure
sold for £360. A set of four teabowls went for £360. A set of eighteen
winecups, gloriously decorated with painted insects hovering above
floral sprigs, went for £330. A pair of unusual blue and white winepots and covers, sold for £500. A kraak porcelain bowl reached £400.
Lot 68 was a blue and white kendi, with a squat, globular body
boldly decorated with birds perched on rocks and with flowering
plants in a continuous scene around the pot. This lovely piece was
sold for £520, almost twice the sum anticipated.

As the sale progressed, it was obvious that the romantic history
of the *Witte Leeuw* porcelain had captured the imagination of
collectors. Within this specialized auction, Sotheby's experts had
gauged their estimated prices exactly right for all items other than
the *Witte Leeuw* porcelain. Often their estimates were one third of
the final price. A set of six Swatow bowls, for instance, estimated at
between £80 and £100, went for £420. A white-glazed jar of a slender
ovoid form about nine inches high, together with a jarlet in similar
glaze, estimated to sell for between £30 and £50, were finally

Spoons, plates and other crested or marked personal items can help enormously in the vital identification of a wreck. These come from a variety of European wrecks.

knocked down for £540. This was no adverse reflection on Sotheby's staff. Wreck auctions broke new ground—no one knew the collectors' value for sure.

Those 49 lots netted £17,000 for Robert Sténuit and the Royal Netherlands Government. Sotheby's had once again established a new collecting vogue and were highly delighted at such a successful sale. Their associated company in Amsterdam had done almost as well, including the disposal of two *Witte Leeuw* bronze cannon. As for Robert Sténuit and his team, a lot of serious-minded collectors are waiting for his next discoveries in the realm of fine art.

Particular to Florida waters are the curious inhabitants that nose their way in as divers search the sea bed, hoping for tasty items of food to be disturbed. (Dave Burrell)

7

In the Scillies with Rex Cowan

With all the publicity created by the Sténuit and Morris diving teams, the mass of speculation printed by national newspapers in England and aired on the radio, it was only natural that a number of like-minded divers and team-leaders would be researching along their own lines. In Holland, at national archives in The Hague and Amsterdam, Zelide Cowan was building up a bulky file on Dutch East Indiamen, lost around the Western Approaches, particularly on the Scillies. Two shipwrecks in particular were of special interest to the Cowans, the *Princesse Maria* and *Hollandia*.

Research in Holland revealed a number of clues that only an on-site investigation could link together. And so Rex Cowan headed for the Scilly Isles to find the *Hollandia*, a VOC ship of the Amsterdam Chamber thought lost on her maiden voyage when carrying a number of chests of newly minted coin from Dutch mints, coin for trade in the East Indies—*Hollandia* was a pay-ship loaded with silver ducatons.

Of all the Chambers that made up the Dutch East India Company, Amsterdam was by far the biggest. Manufacturing and distribution industries turned Holland into the world's leading industrial nation by the mid-1700s. Linens were manufactured in Haarlem; Delft became famous for potteries and breweries, Leiden for its cloths, Gouda for cordage and clay pipes, but Amsterdam was the heart of the industrial upsurge. There were refineries for sugar, salt, pepper, cinnamon, camphor—all from the Spice Islands. There, too, they made velvets and satins and silks, gold and silver brocades, ribbons; there were saw mills for timber, marble polishers, cutters and polishers of diamonds. Ships were needed to carry raw materials to factories and finished goods to markets. Shipbuilders and owners who made up the six Chambers of the VOC built and provisioned the vessels and carried the trade.

Holland relied on the Spice Islands for its prosperity. Huge profits could be made, despite a high percentage of ship losses. A conservative estimate, from examination of VOC files in Amsterdam and Rotterdam, would place annual losses at between twenty and thirty per cent. During one of the early years of trading, out of thirty-seven ships that left Holland only twenty-four returned but, throughout the history of seventeenth and eighteenth century trading, an annual ship loss of twenty per cent was about average. The loss of experienced seamen, particularly officers, was perhaps of greater import than the loss of ships. Shipbuilding became a major industry with the Dutch and wooden sailing ships, designed primarily for bulk storage capacity, regularly left the builders' yards. In 1742 the Amsterdam Chamber alone commissioned seven new ships, *Overnes, Den Heuvel, Hollandia, Hersteller, Eendraght, Wickenburg* and *Adrichem*.

Hollandia, of 750 tons, was about 150 feet in length with a beam of 42 feet; three masts, fore, main and mizzen carried a huge expanse of sail, sorely needed, for the stubby hull forward made close wind sailing next to impossible. The hull design certainly coped with bulk storage of coffee, yet made a costly sacrifice of sea-keeping qualities. By the spring of 1743, she was ready to sail to Batavia, together with the *Overnes* and *Den Heuvel*. There had been worries that a shortage of officers and seamen might delay this convoy's sailing but last minute recruitment brought crews almost up to full strength. Jan Kelder was appointed captain of *Hollandia* for her maiden voyage. This was his second trip as a Master, his fourth altogether. His first mate was Jan Holst, a fine seaman with similar experience of the East Indies route. A crew of 150 men and 80 VOC soldiers finally sailed, as too did a number of important passengers.

Gustav William, Baron von Imhoff, was at that time Governor-General of the Dutch East Indies, and sailing out to join him on the

Film records are vital but not always practical. Here a diver uses a ciné film camera with a strong light to pierce the gloom. (Dave Burrell)

Hollandia was his youngest brother, Hendrik Francois; Hendrik's wife Mechteld Bentinck; her young unmarried sister Anna Bentinck and Anna's maid Margaret Klevering.

Before the Noordzeekanaal was cut to link Amsterdam with the North Sea port of IJmuiden, ships had to sail around the Friesian islands through the Zuiderzee into Amsterdam. When sailing for Batavia, a last provisioning and embarking point would be the port of Den Burg, on the island of Texel. It was from there, on July 3, 1743, that *Hollandia, Overnes* and *Den Heuvel* set sail in convoy for Batavia, pennants and banners streaming as cheering crowds, family and friends waved and shouted 'Goede reis' to the trading venture.

As with all matters concerning the VOC, there are meticulous records appertaining to each Chamber, its vessels, voyages, cargoes and trading instructions. A record exists of every resolution passed by the directors of the VOC. In the Koloniaal Archief at Den Haag, the Maritiem Museum Prins Hendrik in Rotterdam, in the Scheepvaartmuseum and Amsterdams Historisch Museum, in Utrecht, Zeeland and Dordrecht, old papers exist to fill in any gaps. The VOC directed that,

> . . . *ships' masters of the summer fleet travelling from the Netherlands to Batavia . . . shall firstly sail down the Channel and arriving at Land's End or the Lizard, shall set a South-Westerly course to latitude 43° in order to by-pass Cape Finisterre by 60 miles, except when otherwise ordered in written instructions . . .*

So greatly were the financial backers concerned to avoid ship-wreck that, though land-based men, they presumed to set the sails of their ships themselves, as if written instructions were some form of guarantee against the vagaries of storm and pestilence.

Dutch divisional flagship, similar to Hollandia. (Prins Hendrik Maritime Museum)

According to instructions, therefore, the three ships sailed majestically through the English Channel. They were reported seen on July 9 (new calendar) by Captain Jan Boot, inward bound from Bilbao. Between July 9 and 13 a fierce south-westerly gale blew up with heavy rain further hampering visibility. At 6.30 a.m., July 13, Captain Willem Bakker reported sighting two ships two miles south of the Scillies 'in thick weather and heavy seas, the wind to westerly . . .' Captain Bakker heard indistinctly that a ship had been wrecked on the Scillies but 'knew not her name'.

Among Scillonian papers for the year of 1743, a journal published by a Captain Robert Heath, an engineer officer, sent to report on the fortifications of the islands, contains a contemporary account of a wreck that year, although the name is omitted or was not known. Heath wrote:

> . . . *about the year* 1743 *a Dutch East Indiaman outward bound, was lost off St Agnes in about* 20 *or* 22 *fathoms of water, with all the people. Their firing of guns, as a signal of . . . distress, was heard in the night but none could give assistance.*

Another useful account, although clearly second or third hand, came from Parson Troutbeck, known to be on the island of St Mary's in the 1770s, who wrote that 'an unknown Dutch ship . . . struck upon the Gunner Rock in Broad Sound off St Agnes and sank down in about 22 fathoms depth of water . . .'

Although neither Heath nor Troutbeck identified their wreck, sufficient clues existed in Rex Cowan's mind to justify the expense of a full-scale expedition and in 1970 the search for *Hollandia* began. Cowan obtained exclusive rights from the Royal Netherlands Government to search for and salvage where possible items from two VOC ships, the *Princesse Maria*, wrecked in 1686 on Silver Carn in the Scillies, close to Bishop and Clark Rocks, and the *Hollandia*, thought to be the vessel lost on Gunner Rocks.

A glance at the Scillies chart shows clear water for hundreds of yards around Gunner. To the west lie the Crim Rocks, east by a little south the islet of Annet, south the Retarriers; the north lies open and this possibly was *Hollandia*'s course. Perhaps Jan Kelder, finding himself north of the Scillies, had turned south thinking he was clear of the western rocks. He ran, instead, onto the Gunner's. Broad Sound is the channel that runs into the main islands from the south-west. Cowan guessed that, having struck Gunner, *Hollandia* would make for the nearest landmass, that of Annet off St Agnes. Accordingly, Cowan ran a grid square over six square miles east of Gunner, trying to judge the vessel's movements in a south-westerly gale once she had struck and was, presumably, making water. He had to reckon how far she might have run for safety before she foundered and split asunder under the pressure of water in her hull.

Cowan hired a team of divers, a minimum of five augmented at times to eight, and began with a detailed search of the base of Gunner Rock. This produced no evidence of wreck. It was then decided to search an area up to 500 yards east. Once started, the team soon realized how vast the area of sea bed was. They searched by long swims on compass bearings or by fanning out, connected by swim lines; in either case their search depended for success on good visibility. By the end of that July there was still no sign of any wreckage.

Magnetometers had already been used successfully for underwater searches in the United States, so Cowan next cast around for such

A Cowan team diver holds up a Bellarmine jar from the 1686 Princesse Maria *wreck. Such a jar would contain about 35 pounds of mercury used for refining silver. As the Dutch had cornered the European market for mercury, signs of it are always a clue towards a Dutch VOC wreck.* (F. E. Gibson)

an instrument and contacted Anthony Lonsdale, an electronics expert, to gain his support. A magnetometer towed behind a boat produces a graph of the sea bed—any ferrous metal object should produce a reading on the graph. In the event Cowan's first experiment with such a device did not help and, at the end of August, diving was suspended until the next spring. But during the winter tests were carried out using a proton-magnetometer, fitted with sensors capable of overcoming hydrostatic misreadings. In April, 1971, Lieutenant-Commander Jack Gayton R.N., a recently retired Naval diver, led a new team and began a second stage exploration fanning further out towards Annet.

For day after day, week after week they searched and found nothing. Searching the sea bed for wreck traces is often a soul-destroying, bitterly cold experience that requires a constantly high level of optimism fuelled by something tangible, no matter how small. Team diving is also a very expensive business and Cowan had limited financial resources. Still nothing had been found by September. The team were quite understandably at a low ebb of morale. Cowan too was worried. His finances were running out and it appeared that his gamble was lost. The whole team were mentally and physically exhausted.

There were only a few days of the diving season left when, searching an area over 2,000 yards east of Gunner Rock, a reading suddenly appeared on the magnetometer graph. The whole team dived and searched the area the next day and found nothing, a bitter disappointment. Cowan insisted they search the same area the following day, still convinced that he was searching in the right area. The site was directly east from Gunner, precisely on the line along which a stricken vessel would be driven by a westerly wind and precisely, too, on a line for the nearest landmass, Annet.

On September 18, the team went below again. Visibility was poor but cannon, lead ingots and anchors were seen. After such a long period of disappointment it was a very nervy team that waited, sleeping fitfully, for a closer look the next day. They found a bronze cannon with the monogram of the Amsterdam Chamber of the VOC —without doubt it was a Dutch East Indiaman, but they could not be certain it was *Hollandia* for at least seven VOC ships have been wrecked around the Scillies. It was vital that Cowan proved the wreck's identity, before a hoard of scavenging divers descended

upon the site. Divers had already been observed watching the movements and activities of the Cowan team.

It was a silver spoon with a crest on it that provided the necessary
proof. The crest was a prince's crown surmounting two circlets, the
left depicting a lion and quartered by seals, the right showing a
Jerusalem Cross—the arms of the Imhoff-Bentinck family. There
was no doubt that the wreck was that of the *Hollandia*. But there
was just time for the team's well-deserved elation to be crowned by
a last breathtaking find.

On almost the last day of the diving season, two team members
suddenly came upon a mound of rock more than ten feet high
and about twelve feet around, a curious, unnatural protuberance
on the sea bed. They made a closer inspection, chipping away the
seagrowth, and revealed to their amazement that the entire mound
was made up of thousands of calcified silver coins. When they surfaced and shouted their news, no one believed them, and the whole
team insisted on going below to inspect what from then on was
known as 'Silver Hill'. A few specimen coins were chipped away for
a detailed examination. It had always been known that the
Hollandia had been carrying silver to Batavia but how much silver
could only be guessed. For reasons of security the VOC cargo mani-
fests rarely listed bullion or gold or silver coin, other than ship's
money, crews' wages and the like. No one had anticipated 'Silver
Hill'!

Back in his lodgings in St Mary's, Rex Cowan cleaned and in-
spected the samples. There were newly minted 1743 silver ducatons
from Overijssel and Utrecht mints, delivered directly to *Hollandia*
for Batavia—unique coins, known as 'Silver Riders' by the obverse
knight on horseback. It was a find that came just in time for Rex
Cowan's depleted finances. Eventually more than 35,000 coins were
retrieved from *Hollandia*. If a conservative figure of £30 is placed
upon the worth of each coin then *Hollandia* was without doubt a
£1,000,000 wreck.

But in that September, 1971, this fortune was still on the sea bed
and Cowan already knew of the continuing rape and pillage by
Roland Morris's rivals on the *Association*. He had to ensure that his
own rights were protected on the *Hollandia*. Accordingly, he advised the Dutch Government, who owned the wreck, of his discovery, and also informed H.M. Receiver of Wreck, Scilly Isles. He

A siege mortar carried on board Hollandia *by the VOC militia for use on land or for firing blazing projectiles if in action at sea. Like bronze cannon, the lifting eyes were cast in the form of gambolling dolphins.* (F. E. Gibson)

attached a buoy to the wreck and extensively advertised that he was 'Diver in Possession' and would take immediate legal action against anyone trespassing.

Despite these endeavours, Rex Cowan was faced with exactly the same problems that Roland Morris and Robert Sténuit had battled against. Moreover, his marker buoy was moored to, of all things, the Silver Hill! Following clandestine looting, Cowan, a solicitor himself, moved into litigation with injunctions against a number of divers which were upheld and a court case against two other divers that resulted in the return of a couple of hundred filched coins and two heavy fines against the culprits. This unfortunate business brought home to Cowan what Roland Morris had realized several years previously, that a new law to protect historic wrecks was long overdue. Enthusiastically he gave his support to progress in that direction provided by the stimulus of Roland Morris and John Nott, Member of Parliament for St Ives.

That winter, Cowan began to plan for the next diving season and considered the historic value of artifacts that would be retrieved from the wreck-site. He determined to carry out, as far as was practical, a full archaeological survey of the *Hollandia* wreck. He was also thinking ahead to the second of his Dutch East Indiamen, the *Princesse Maria* which foundered on the Scillies in 1686. This wreck had a special place in history for it was plundered by a reigning monarch—James II of England.

By using the improved proton magnetometer once again, in his attempt to locate the *Princesse Maria*, Rex Cowan undertook a huge search area and, in the region of Silver Carn, his divers found wreck remains. Utilizing the search survey pattern as they did when locating the *Hollandia*, the divers quickly came upon a number of artifacts that established the wreck's identity as the *Princesse Maria*. The Amsterdam motif of the VOC was clear upon many spoons. There was also a bellermine flagon, still corked and still with its contents of 40 lb of mercury intact after 287 years beneath the sea. *Princesse Maria* had been outward-bound from Texel to Batavia and, amongst its cargo, was loaded a quantity of mercury, a commodity then used in silver refining.

Before the mid-1500s the main method of refining silver was simply by smelting the lead ore. A German process of amalgamation with mercury came into common use around 1550, using mercury to separate silver from base metal. In such a process, poorer quality silver ore could be mined and refined. This was important because, the poorer the grade, the less silver ore could be obtained through ordinary smelting. Therefore mercury became the key ingredient in silver production throughout the world. Dutch traders moved quickly to obtain sole trading rights to Austrian mercury production. In consequence, mercury traces are often found in VOC wrecks.

To the casual observer this may appear as a mildly interesting piece of information about the processes of sixteenth and seventeenth century silver production. But to the treasure hunter such information becomes a vital clue towards the identification of a Dutch VOC merchantman. Mercury traces on the seabed meant the strong possibility of a Dutchman outward-bound; being outward-bound, she might well be a pay-ship; being a pay-ship, the divers knew they should keep their eyes open for oxidised pieces-of-eight. So the logic ran.

Rex Cowan knew the significance of the contents of the bellermine jar. But he was not all that surprised when his team, surveying
as best they could in that difficult region of the Silver Carn, found
only a few coins. The *Princesse Maria* had reputedly been well
'rummaged' in the past and had been the subject of a considerable
diplomatic exchange.

History records that the *Princesse Maria* remained above water
for a few weeks after being wrecked, long enough for the Scillonians,
experts at clearing a wreck of her valuables, to take their pickings.
The Lord Protector of the Scillies, one Sir Francis Godolphin, who
resided on St Mary's Island, held within his manorial and protector
rights all items of wreck. These provided a regular income in the
Scillies, with its hundreds of rocks, reefs and small islands. But such
rights, when there was actual coin, had to be shared with the
monarch, James II.

On receiving word of a providential wreck, James dispatched his
own yacht *Isabella* to the islands with as much circumspection as
possible and received from Godolphin a consignment of plundered
coin to the amount of 13,000 pieces-of-eight. This clandestine
operation naturally took time. Within days of the wrecking, the
Dutch East India Company applied to the High Court of the
Admiralty to protect their rights and allow Dutch salvage operations to commence. Letters passed with increasing animosity between the Dutch Ambassador, James II, Lord Middleton (the
Secretary of State) and Samuel Pepys, then Secretary to the
Admiralty.

James was already aware that the House of Orange threatened to
depose him. His daughter and her husband, William of Orange, were
making ready to cross over to England and James was in no mood
for co-operation. He delayed answering the Dutch requests, pro-
crastinating long and successfully until he received word from
Godolphin that the coins were successfully transferred; not until
October, ten months after the *Princesse Maria* had been driven onto
Silver Carn, did James angrily instruct Samuel Pepys to issue an
order: 'Commanding his Admirals, Captains and the Crown's
Servants to do all in their power to assist the Dutch in recovering
their property from the wreck.' The wreck, by that time, had been
pounded to a pulp and such remains as there were lay fathoms deep
below Silver Carn.

In consequence, Cowan's pickings nearly three centuries later proved meagre, but this was offset by the first public auction of items recovered from the *Hollandia*, which had already been sold by Sotheby's with great success.

The great Admiral's lowly chamber pot made of pewter. Sold by Sotheby's for £270. When cleaning inside the curled rim Morris found two gold coins embedded. Each coin was worth more than £300! (Sotheby Parke Bernet & Co.)

The interest of collectors, having been aroused by the original *Association* auction, had been sustained in the second *Association* sale at which prices were considerably higher. For example, Lot number 107, a Portuguese 4,000 reis of 1705, very fine and scarce, sold for £310. The silver plate with Sir Cloudesley Shovell's crest upon it, the very plate that had finally proved the identity of *Association*, went for a high £2,100. And amidst great cheering, a very bent and battered relic—a rare pewter chamber pot reputed to have been the personal property of the Admiral himself—sold for £270. When Sotheby's announced they would be auctioning some of the coins and other artifacts recovered from *Hollandia* they were

Pieces-of-Eight. In lot 195 you can see the irregular shaped hand-stamped silver Cob coins, before machine-milled coins of 1732. This Cob sold for £22. Lot 221, however, sold for £650. Some machine-minted coins appear to have been clipped off, a common practice of payment when the debt did not reach the full value of the coin. (Sotheby Parke Bernet & Co.)

therefore already assured of considerable interest. On April 18, 1972, Sotheby's New Bond Street galleries were packed with buyers not only from the United Kingdom and Holland but from Germany, France, United States, Scandinavia and Japan.

The sale began quietly and the first lot of three Brabant minted ducatons of 1618 and 1619 sold for £32. But it did not take long for prices to rise. Two half-ducatons of 1649 and 1665, described as 'about fair and rare', were sold after hectic bidding for £250. A later lot, eleven Flanders ducatons of 1670 and 1673, with a description only 'fair', sold for £290. Good though such prices were, it was Lot numbers 221–226 that caused the real buzz of conversation around the hall.

'Two hundred and twenty-one—hold it up please', said the auctioneer in an aside to one of the porters.

'A pillar dollar eight reales of Philip the Fifth. A Mexico City mint dated 1732—of significance, ladies and gentlemen, the year of the first machine milled coins from the New World—this coin is good and rare.'

He paused and looked around the room.

'At two hundred can we begin—thank you', his searching eyes had caught a bid.

'Two hundred and fifty—and three hundred—and fifty—four hundred, thank you—four fifty—five hundred, yes? and fifty . . . and seventy-five? Yes, at five hundred and seventy-five . . . six hundred . . . and twenty-five, thank you, sir, at six hundred and twenty-five, . . . against you . . . six hundred and fifty, thank you, at six hundred and fifty then . . .' He took a brief moment to glance around and then slammed down an ebony hammer upon his rostrum desk, 'Six hundred and fifty pounds.' He murmured a name to his clerk. It was a good price for a single coin.

The next lot, a pillar eight reales of 1733, classed 'very fine and rare', went for £640; another of the same date and 'fine and rare', went for £520. Altogether that morning, the sale of coins brought in a total of £20,227, and there was still the afternoon auction to come.

By the time the last lot of the sale, Lot 503, was called, it was a very satisfied team of divers who listened to the bidding for a fine Dutch bronze cannon by Claude Fremy of Amsterdam, cast in 1694 and bearing in relief the monogram of the Amsterdam Chamber of the Vereenigde Oostindische Compagnie VOC. Bidding was brisk and the cannon was finally knocked down at £2,000.

The afternoon sale raised £17,126, making a grand total for the day of £37,353. After sale expenses and the Dutch Government's share Rex Cowan was left with an amount that covered his expenses so far with some over for his current plans. For his diving team of Jack Gayton, Nowell Pearce, Terry Hiron and Jim Heslin, and for his boat skipper David Stedeford and for Anthony Lonsdale, who had supplied the magnetometer, and for all the researchers, it had been a great day—rewarding financially and rewarding too in the considerable interest shown in their activities. They all looked forward to the coming diving season with renewed hope and endeavour. Forgotten were the hours of bone-chilling cold, the currents, the poachers; they remembered, rather, the first sight of 'Silver Hill'. The first auction of *Hollandia* items was very well celebrated that night!

8

Sir William Hamilton's Priceless Pottery

Following the first auction of the *Association* and the difficulties encountered in proving identification of the wreck, Roland Morris was to turn his attention on the rest of Sir Cloudesley Shovell's squadron that had been lost: *Eagle, Romney* and *Firebrand*.

It was only reluctantly that he abandoned the *Association*. Proving its identification had not solved his problems as to the protection of his legal rights and much of his time was subsequently spent in championing a new law for the protection of historic wrecks. That law, known as the Protection of Wrecks Act 1973, finally came on to the Statute Book in July of next year. This was the protection so badly needed and so long fought for by Morris and the Member of Parliament for St Ives in Cornwall, John Nott, among many others. Yet, paradoxically, the one site that high-lighted the need for the protection of historic wrecks, the *Association*, dynamited and plundered for its treasure, never obtained the Secretary of State's order. To this day *Association* lies unprotected by the 1973 Act. Despite pleas to reconsider, the Minister stands obdurate. The official position is that, after years of plundering on the *Association* wreck site, there can be nothing left of historic interest. Yet every diving day upon *Association* still brings up something of interest.

There was, for example, the notable discovery made in July 1973, the same month as the enactment of the new Protection Act. Two excellent divers had arrived to take up residence in the Scillies, Terry Hiron and Jim Heslin. Terry Hiron had been a member of Bob Rogers team, one of the original M.O.D. licensed divers for the *Association* wreck. And it was diving beneath the Gilstone accompanied by another diver, Don Bates, that Hiron and Heslin made an outstanding discovery. They simply moved a giant iron cannon out of the way and there, beneath, lay a carpet of neatly lined coins, 8,000 to be exact. There were crowns, half-crowns and shillings with rare dates of Charles II, James II and William III; there were also Spanish New World cobs and pieces-of-eight. Yet despite such a find, there was still no protection for the *Association*.

With the original M.O.D. licence now expired, Hiron and Heslin, who clearly still wished to work the *Association* having just made a staggering find, had to resort to the old Shipping Act and were registered as 'salvors in possession', buoying the wreck and advertising legal action against everyone found trespassing. As for the Morris team, all the controversy, the bickering—and even fighting and dynamiting—had proved too much. His team left *Association* to others and set out to find the rest of Sir Cloudesley's ships that were wrecked that dark night in 1707.

When looking back on the *Association* saga, a number of disquieting thoughts intrude. From the very beginning those in authority were reluctant to confirm the identity of the wreck despite a wealth of circumstantial evidence. There have been occasions since, when identification of wrecks has been allowed on far scantier proof; indeed, one particular site has been designated on the evidence of cannon of dubious dating. The Secretary of State acts upon the recommendations of a committee set up under the chairmanship of Lord Runciman. Many of this committee are eminent historians and archaeologists including a number with a maritime interest.

There is no doubt that the pillaging, plunder and indiscriminate use of explosives on the *Association* site was criminal, both in law and from the archaeological point of view, yet it would seem to many that the few who acted quite within the law and attempted, under extremely hazardous conditions, some form of intelligent survey, have been tainted with the tar-brush of suspicion because

Mark Horobin, Mike Hicks and Colin Gregory after a cold dive on the Romney. (Benbow/Morris Collection)

of the illegal actions of others. There are those who might think that this could well be a case of tit-for-tat by academic archaeologists rapping the knuckles of those more artisan by profession who admit to being treasure hunters as well as holding an interest in marine archaeology. It is to be hoped that those who think thus are wrong.

After all, it is the professed treasure hunter who provides the glamour and the publicity—as well as substantial amounts of money to the country or authority who legally own such wreck—that attracts the sort of attention to the subject that often enables the pure archaeologist to raise the necessary funds for his or her work. Robert Sténuit makes no secret of his love of treasure. Yet donating hundreds of artifacts to the Ulster Museum was a totally generous, unsolicited act that has enabled thousands who, for various reasons—age, health and so on—are unable to dive, to experience for themselves history beneath the sea.

Roland Morris himself has built and maintains at his own expense a museum of nautical art in Penzance, crammed full of wonderful artifacts from West Country wrecks. A joy for many schoolparties and tourists. Rex Cowan finds time to serve on the Runciman Committee. All three—Sténuit, Morris and Cowan—are keen treasure seekers yet prove tangibly their true love for historical fact. And still there are those within the marine archaeological field who turn up their noses at the professional diver who takes considerable risks to reclaim artifacts of great historical note.

In effect driven off the *Association*, Roland Morris first directed his team's efforts into searching for the 50-gun *Romney*, known to have perished on Tearing Ledges in about 70 feet of water. *Romney* was found exactly where Morris thought the wreck would lie and his team recovered, intact, a marvellous bronze ship's bell, presented by the town of Romney in 1701, which has been cleaned and polished as new. Morris attempted a brief survey and retrieved an iron cannon. A few other artifacts were brought up from the wreck before other divers decided *Romney*, too, was fair game.

Rather than risk his divers in the punch-up that often ensued when rival teams dived on the same wreck, Morris moved on to the 70-gun *Eagle*, that split asunder on the Crim Rocks. Again Morris was successful and for once his team had the wreck to themselves, for the *Eagle* lies 165 feet down and not many of the 'poachers' relish such a depth.

Roland Morris recovered from the *Eagle* a wardroom bell badly affected by bronze disease, a bronze sheave with the broad arrow mark of the Royal Navy; copper sheet remnants (this metal was often used for hot water boilers, which were sited forward under the forecastle of a ship where a large brick fire-place heated the boiler or giant kettles for hot water cooking); copper spikes; a pair of ship's navigational dividers; a bronze hand gun; and a few coins including a magnificent eight-escudo piece, alone worth some £2000 today.

The *Eagle* wreck site proved interesting in many ways, not least for her final resting place. In hitting a section of the Crim Rocks, the ship split into three pieces. The first came to rest at the base of the Crim, the middle section near Zantmans Rock and the third piece off North Rock, all within the Crim reef. Several hundred yards separate the first from the third section of the wreck. *Eagle* struck the Crim bow-on, heading on a north-easterly course, being

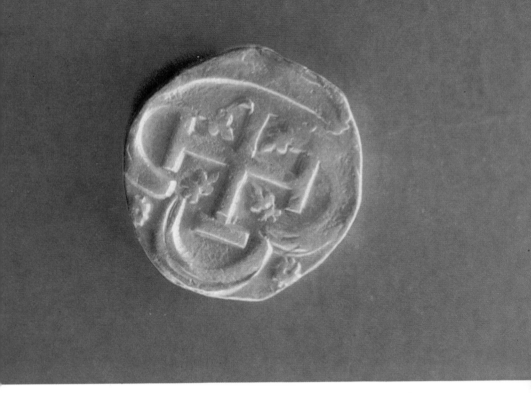

The fabulous gold escudo from the wreck of the Romney—*worth around £2,000 at 1980 prices.* (Benbow/Morris Collection)

driven by a west-sou'west gale. Morris deduced that, once struck, *Eagle*'s stern swung to port, her bow section broke off, followed by her middle section and finally her stern section sank, making up the three wreck sites.

Site number one had revealed two huge anchors and one smaller, twenty-one cannon and the badly damaged wardroom bell. On site number two, the divers had spotted some coins, two medium guns and ten smaller guns (these were close together, as though being carried as cargo or stores for other ships or as ground siege pieces. There was also some English silver, the dividers and bowl sherds of seventeenth century pottery. Four large cannon and a large stern anchor were located at the third site.

Many of the iron cannon had typical sea growth, a calcified concretion that forms on iron items by a combination of chemical and microscopic marine life. A guide to the length of time such items have been in the sea can be gleaned by the thickness of this 'crud' growth. Some of *Eagle*'s guns had a thickness of several inches.

There was enough evidence below the Crim to suggest that the remains of *Eagle* were not the only wreck items below that reef. Other ship's artifacts may yet be recovered from the Crim. So prolific were the wrecks on certain particularly hazardous shoals that one wreck lies upon another as on sections of the Goodwin Sands. Perhaps one day a full inspection will be made but first the new Act to Protect Historic Wrecks should be used to have the Crim designated as a restricted diving area. At least *Romney* now has such protection and the Tearing Ledge is a restricted and designated site.

Finally Morris located *Firebrand*, the fourth ship lost from Sir Cloudesley Shovell's fleet. As her name suggests, she had been a fireship, a small vessel; indeed, so little remained on her site between Annet and St Agnes islands that it was not even considered practical to conduct a survey. Whilst his team were active below, Morris continued his researches into another historic giant that foundered somewhere in the Scillies in the year 1798. HMS *Colossus*, a vessel of Nelson's fleet, had carried a cargo of priceless Greek and Etruscan pottery, part of a collection belonging to Sir William Hamilton.

It is an irony of history that many august personalities who are worth remembering for their own accomplishments suffer in relation to less worthy but more spectacular contemporaries. So it was in the case of Sir William Hamilton, British Envoy Extraordinary to King Ferdinand of Naples and Sicily from 1786 to 1800. History, in passing, records him more often as the cuckolded husband of Emma, the vivacious mistress of Admiral Lord Nelson.

But Sir William Hamilton is worthy of more than a passing notoriety. Apart from being an extremely able diplomat, he was an acknowledged expert on volcanoes, and was able to observe nearby Vesuvius in all its varying moods and eruptions. After writing a number of scholarly papers on the subject, he was elected a Fellow of the Royal Society. Passionate though his interest was in Vesuvius, his real interest and scholarship lay in ancient Greek and Etruscan pottery, marvellously painted pots, vases, bell kators and bowls of the period from 700 to 400 BC. With Herculaneum and Pompeii close by, Sir William began to amass a wonderful collection by judicious bargaining and bartering. He also collected paintings by Rubens, Tintoretto, Titian, Canaletto and other masters.

Although Hamilton was related to the Duke of Hamilton, his personal fortune hardly sustained his elegant mode of life, with the endless entertaining his position in the Court of King Ferdinand demanded. Like all diplomats of the day—ambassadors and pleni-potentiaries—the honour of position was greater than the hope of an equally honourable salary. For the whole period of Hamilton's residence in Naples, his lack of real fortune concerned him greatly. A loving first wife had brought to the marriage a small estate in Wales and the income, though modest, had been very important. Cultured, although of delicate disposition, Hamilton's first wife was a strong support, a view often confirmed in Sir William's letters to his rather dilettante nephew, Charles Greville, on whose behalf Hamilton frequently bought paintings and marbles.

By 1780 Sir William had built up an outstanding collection of Greek and Etruscan treasures. Returning home for a well earned leave, and for his wife to receive medical attention, he sold that first collection to the British Museum for the sum of £8,400. His depleted fortune was somewhat restored and the British Museum had begun what would turn out many years and many acquisitions later to be the world's outstanding collection of Greek pottery.

Hamilton's visit to London enabled him to confer many times with his nephew Greville at the latter's house in Paddington Green, there to be entertained at tea by his nephew's mistress, Emma. The young girl was beautiful and eager to improve herself, at all times willing to attend to Greville's every whim, for he had taken her in when with child after she had been thrown out of a certain baronet's house destitute and helpless. Sir William was to remember Emma a few years later.

Back in Naples Hamilton began to lay the foundations of his second collection, which he always described in letters to Greville as 'much superior to that now lying with the British Museum'. Not only did he believe the design of the pots and vases to be of classic beauty but he was also confident that their decoration—the paintings depicting ancient gods, Bacchanalian revelry and animals —were of the very finest artistry and draughtsmanship.

As this second collection grew so to did Sir William's need to sell it for a high price. Alas, his collecting prospered but his loyal and faithful wife died, leaving a sore gap in his life. His letters to Greville spoke of his great loneliness, a point Greville was happy

Roland Morris in the Great Cabin of the Nautical Museum, Penzance, looking at a sectional model of an English man-o'war. (Benbow/Morris Collection)

to rectify. He himself was casting around for a rich wife and an incumbent mistress did not lend a good tone to his background. He wrote to his uncle suggesting that the good Emma could keep house for Sir William. The matter was agreed upon. Emma went to Hamilton, leaving Greville free.

At first, Emma did run the house in Naples for Sir William; later she shared his bed. Still later, she became his second wife. It seemed an unlikely combination—the aristocratic, elderly Hamilton, thin and with a scholarly appearance, and the young voluptuous Emma. But she looked after the increasingly frail diplomat and left him in peace with the beloved pots, paintings and pottery that he gathered about him in his fine house in plenty.

In 1791, aware that this would be the last collection he was likely to gather together and requiring to sell it for a good sum,

Disorientation at depth is always a problem for divers, hence the use of a long-line for safety. (Dave Burrell)

Deep Sea Treasure

Hamilton commissioned the Director of the Naples Art Gallery, Wilhelm Tischbein, to draw a series of folios showing the beauty of pots, vases, kators and their exquisite paintings. Two hundred years later, Hamilton's idea of preserving a form of catalogue of his collection turned out to be an unforeseen stroke of good fortune. Tischbein laboured on this Gargantuan task for three years, for there were several hundred items to be drawn. At last, when the commission was accomplished, the folios were sent overland, first to the King of Prussia, who had indicated possible interest in acquiring such a collection, and then to London, where they ended up in the British Museum.

By the late 1790s the political situation had deteriorated in Italy and Napoleon's forces were moving towards Naples. Until then, the presence of Nelson's squadron had kept the French at bay but by 1798 it seemed nothing would keep them from Naples. The Court of Ferdinand therefore decided to evacuate Naples for Palermo, on Sicily. Hastily, Hamilton arranged for his valuable collection to be crated—so hastily in fact, that no true record was kept of the contents of the eighteen huge crates. Prevailing upon his friendship

Matching a Colossus *sherd to a superbly accurate Tischbein drawing.* (Benbow/Morris Collection)

with Nelson, Hamilton requested that his crates be dispatched to England on the next available ship. Part of the collection, thought to be twelve crates, was loaded upon HMS *Colossus*, due back in England for refitting; the balance was loaded upon Nelson's own *Foudroyant*.

There was no doubt of the friendship between Hamilton and Nelson. The young commodore admired the old diplomat's courtly style and Sir William clearly tolerated the relationship between Nelson and Emma, for by now he was an old man grown more frail with the passage of time; the attraction of a young wife had palled somewhat and her demands upon his strength and attention were often wearing. In addition, the worsening political situation pressed fresh demands on an already tired old man.

The house in Naples was closed up and Sir William Hamilton's crates began their journey home to England, safe in the holds of HMS *Colossus*, captained by a personal friend of Nelson, Captain George Murrey. This was a somewhat disillusioned officer, un-enamoured of his ship, eager to return to England for a new command that might make up for the past few years with its doleful lack of honour and prize-money. For Murrey, *Colossus* had not lived up to the promise of glory for which he had hoped.

Colossus was not an old ship by any means. She had been built at Southwark in 1787. Her class, with 74 guns, was much favoured by Nelson, for they were fast and highly manoeuvrable in comparison with other ships of that time. But *Colossus* was only a shadow of her former self. During the battle of Cape St Vincent, she had been chosen to lead the British attack on the French fleet. Unfortunately, the French Admiral judged to a nicety the very moment that Murrey turned to bring his guns to bear. It was *Colossus* herself who received a well aimed broadside which raked her, causing great damage and carrying away her steering yards. No longer manoeuvrable, she was pulled out of the battle, thereby depriving her captain of any share in the prize-money. *Colossus* was never the same ship again. Although repaired in Gibraltar, continuing service in the Mediterranean only weakened her timbers.

At the Battle of the Nile, at Aboukir Bay, *Colossus* was delegated as storeship, a chore George Murrey hated and a chore that, in part, led to the ship's ultimate fate. Nelson had opened the Battle of the Nile audaciously. Having discovered the French fleet at anchor off

The Colossus *diving team preparing to go below.* (Benbow/Morris Collection)

Aboukir, Nelson led his fleet, under cover of dusk, between the French and the land. Anchoring up for the night, he gave orders to his Captains that just before dawn they should cut their cables and join battle with the French. History records a great victory; what it does not record is that after the battle *Colossus*, as storeship, had to provide many anchors, cables and warps to replace those left on the bottom of Aboukir Bay!

Nelson's fleet returned in part to Gibraltar, in part to Naples where Nelson's wounds were tended by Emma. Some of the Nile wounded were transferred to *Colossus*, when orders came for the ship to return to England for refitting. Sir William Hamilton's crates were added to the cargo and, finally, in October, 1798, Captain George Murrey left Naples bound for Gibraltar, Lisbon and England.

At Lisbon, Murrey found orders awaiting him from Lord St Vincent instructing him to convoy home any British vessel requiring protection from the French. Already three such vessels were waiting for a man o'war escort and another four were in the process of loading. But Murrey would not wait. He no longer trusted *Colossus* as a weather ship and wished to return home before the worst of the winter storms. He wrote despatches to Lord St Vincent explaining his dilemma and sailed for England alone the first day of December.

Colossus made good time until reaching the Western Approaches, where a south-westerly gale increased, forcing Murrey to run for shelter towards the Scillies. *Colossus* sailed up Broad Sound with just enough sail to steer her and anchored off Sampson and St Mary's Island. Men were constantly working pumps to contain the level of water seeping into her bilges. On the night of December 10, with the gale now raging at storm force, *Colossus* began to drag her anchors. The wind had changed to south-easterly and the rocky shore of Sampson lay close. Murrey caused more anchors to be spliced to warps and lowered but to no avail. All the stores—the good anchors, the sound warps—had been issued after Aboukir Bay

A line drawing of Colossus
by Roland Morris.

and what Murrey had left was insufficient. Anchors broke off, cables and warps parted and, at the height of the storm, *Colossus* was forced on to Southward Well Rocks off Sampson. There she quickly began to break up.

Helped by the islanders of Sampson, Murrey began to get his men ashore. Miraculously, only one life was lost; even the wounded on board were saved. The following day some cargo was removed but within a few hours *Colossus* had been pounded to pieces. With her, to the bottom of Southward Well Rocks, went Sir William Hamilton's priceless collection of Greek and Etruscan pottery, marvellous paintings and marble busts. It was a disaster that Sir William could never forget, consoled only fractionally by Wilhelm Tischbein's drawings. His anguish was public knowledge and led cruel cynics of the day to observe that 'Sir William Hamilton lost his wife to an Admiral and his treasures to the sea'. The loss of his treasure certainly weighed more heavily upon him than his wife's association with Nelson. He lived only a few years after the *Colossus* wreck, little knowing that his beloved pottery would eventually reach England.

This was the new treasure that the Roland Morris team sought and they logged up almost two hundred diving hours over two seasons, searching for *Colossus*—'the big one'. The remains of *Colossus* did not in fact lie too deep; at most they were perhaps twenty to fifty feet down. The reason that the wrecksite remained hidden for so long was because of a thick bed of kelp weed six to nine feet long that covered most of the site area, growing from the lower reefs of the Southward Well. Below that again lay a tumbled mass of rocks and gullies and then a seabed of rock and sand. It was there that Roland Morris set his team of three divers, Mark Horobin, Mike Hicks and Slim MacDonnell to search for the *Colossus*.

Their first sighting was of a large bower anchor jammed into the reef, then a second, smaller anchor and then another anchor—each one of a pattern used by the Royal Navy in Nelson's time. The team extended their search area and mapped and charted a section of sea floor that showed up seventeen Royal Navy cannons, two carronades and other items including an intact glass bottle with the seal of GR—George Rex. It was these and other artifacts that convinced Roland Morris they had found the *Colossus*. But what of Sir William Hamilton's treasures?

Yet again the search area was extended to discover the extremes of the wrecksite. It was a considerable task but the first rough survey had been completed when MacDonnell made the vital find— a piece of pottery about three inches by four decorated with the plump-cheeked, curly-haired face of a Grecian child, a small broken piece from a vase or bowl that had been made several centuries before Christ and had lain on the sea bed for 178 years.

The sherd was carefully wrapped and sent to London. Confirmation came almost by return—it was Greek, it was old and it was certainly part of Sir William Hamilton's collection lost when *Colossus* was wrecked in 1798. How could the British Museum be so sure? Quite clearly, in one of their Tischbein folios, there was the same child's face that MacDonnell had found. Sir William Hamilton's prudence had brought its reward at last. The British Museum were delighted, if the diving team could bring up sherds thought to be lying on the sea bed in their thousands, the nightmarish jig-saw could be successfully matched against the Tischbein drawings and the pottery itself might be pieced together again—if the Morris team could find every single piece!

But Roland Morris had another problem first—security and protection for his find. The *Colossus* remains lay in relatively shallow water and the team was well experienced in the depredations of poachers. It was time to put into use the new Protection of Historic Wrecks Act. Morris made application for a licence to protect the* *Colossus* as an historic wreck and for his team to be named on that licence as the only divers permitted to work the designated site. The Secretary of State to the Board of Trade and Industry agreed and the *Colossus* and the Southward Well Rocks remain a restricted area for divers. At last, Roland Morris had an unencumbered site of his own.

When the British Museum asked if he could recover 'every piece of pottery', that is exactly what they meant; not only pieces as large as a hand, but also minute sherds half the size of a small fingernail. In compiling a jig-saw puzzle, it is the one missing piece— no matter how large the puzzle or how small the piece, that stands out with awkward clarity. If it was at all possible, every sherd had to be found.

There was another problem, a human one. None of the experts at the British Museum had any experience of diving conditions in the Western Approaches. This unfortunately led to considerable

*More than 2,000 years old and the artist's work, after 200 years in
the sea, is still preserved. A glowing piece of* Colossus *pottery.*
(Benbow/Morris Collection)

friction between the academic historians and the practical divers.
When team members wished to bring to the surface certain artifacts,
arguments broke out and the academics insisted that all items seen
below should remain *in situ* until a full, detailed survey had charted
everything in its original place.

The divers pleaded in vain with the director sent down to the
Scillies to oversee the surveying and excavation operations. They
explained the problems of sea bed movement, of rolling boulders,
rock-falls, currents and tides. All this fell, at first, on deaf ears.
According to the academics, surveying and excavation followed an
agreed archaeological pattern, whether that excavation took place
on dry land or in the sea, and that pattern must be maintained. A
blistering row brought each side's opinions into the open and from
that point on the situation improved.

The divers had bitterly resented being treated either like children

Mark Horobin surfaces with a large sherd from Colossus. *Island of Sampson in the rear.* (Benbow/Morris Collection)

or ignorant 'heavies' by people totally without experience of the conditions in which they had to work; the cold, the weed, the surging currents. Their point of view was that when they spotted an artifact or sherd, they wished to place it in their retrieval bags at once, knowing full well that, with the varied sea bed activity, the item might be lost to the next tide. For the director, on the other hand, accurate charting was vital to the piecing together of the sherds and the project was of such excitement and importance that the final objective clouded judgement of human considerations. Each side was expert in its particular field of endeavour and, while the divers respected and acknowledged the academics' scholarship regarding Greek and Etruscan art, they were at first disappointed that a reciprocal respect was not accorded to their expertise in discovering and then retrieving the sherds.

It was an exhausting period, diving up to four hours each day in water temperatures that reduced fit, active, men to many minutes of uncontrollable shivering when they surfaced. Even thick neoprene wetsuits could not prevent the near-agony of thawing out, face features swollen and numbed by the intense cold. Section by section the seabed was cleared, charted and then searched for any retrievable item. Kelp weed had to be cut away by hand, a hard job in itself for the hold-fast roots of kelp become anchored to the reefs with surprising strength. Small spades and sifting trays were used so that the tiniest piece of pottery would not be missed. No automatic clearance mechanism could be used for fear of harming the pottery or the painting on the sherds in some way. To the great credit of the divers, they apparently missed precious little.

That first season also involved a detailed survey. More than 8,500 separate pieces of pottery were recovered. Sherds of distinctive red or black vases decorated with superb figures, faces and animals; a flute-playing Pan; a centaur ridden by a drunken reveller; traditional bacchanalian scenes, of wonderful clarity still. There was pottery that originally ranged from compact vases of six inches to more than three feet high; there were wine mixing jars, bell kators and vases of all types. To preserve such glorious work, Roland Morris constructed in his laboratory in Penzance a series of shallow wooden trays with constant flowing fresh water to soak out the salts from the precious pottery. The whole project was supervised by the British Museum. At the end of that first season's diving the washed

Roland Morris painstakingly washing Colossus *sherds free of salts. Sherds from palm to fingernail size all receive the same careful treatment before being sent to the British Museum.* (Daily Telegraph)

sherds were carefully packed up and sent by road to London, where the British Museum sent a police car to escort the historic load from the city's outskirts. No chances were taken on losing this precious collection again.

The costs of such a concerted and arduous diving project were high. Morris as usual contributed a substantial sum himself, while the British Museum lent a good percentage of the total, declaring their intention to attempt a purchase of the whole diving proceeds once the Receiver of Wreck was ready to organize a sale. Ten thousand pounds were expended on the first season of *Colossus* work.

Throughout the winter of 1975/6, everybody connected with the enterprise, from divers to the British Museum staff, kept their fingers crossed, fearful of what damage the winter storms would do. The first chore was to clear the fresh grown kelp weed and re-establish the wrecksite, as the turbulent seas of winter had once more rearranged the sea bed. This year the team were more experienced than before, and knew how and where to check for sherds. By the end of the 1977 diving season almost 30,000 sherds had been recovered, washed and collated at the British Museum. A team of volunteers were engaged on what was undoubtedly the world's most ambitious jig-saw puzzle, with the scale drawings of Wilhelm Tischbein to help them. It has been estimated that almost 250 vases are in various states of completion. The whole is a monumental task but in historic and indeed in financial terms, the potential rewards are priceless.

9

Costs and Rewards

There have, of course, been many divers at work not only in British and European waters but all over the world in the last ten years. They have not all achieved the publicity accorded some of the dramatic finds of Wagner, Morris, Sténuit and Cowan. But their discoveries have often been only a little less remarkable and have certainly been of considerable interest to marine archaeologists and historians. No book of this nature would present a correct picture of the world of underwater treasure hunting that did not include some of the success stories of these enthusiasts.

In Europe, for example, a great number of wrecks have been discovered. The patient and persistent Sidney Wignall was largely instrumental in identifying and surveying three Spanish wrecks of the 1588 Armada. Off the south-west coast of Ireland, in Blasket Sound, assisted by Colin Martin of the Institute of Maritime Archaeology at the University of St Andrews, Wignall identified the *Santa Maria de la Rosa*. Off Fair Isle between the Shetlands and Orkneys, he identified the *El Gran Grifon*. Back in Ireland, it was the turn of *La Trinidad Valencera* in Kinnagoe Bay, county Donegal. Both Wignall and Martin have added considerably to the depth of knowledge about the Spanish Armada of 1588.

On the Outer Skerries, off the Shetlands, Anthony Lonsdale's company, Scientific Survey and Location Ltd, found the wreck of a

Dutch East Indiaman, *De Liefde,* another VOC ship, carrying silver bullion for the Company's trading ventures in the Far East. She was wrecked in 1711, a year in which the normal passage through the English Channel was more than a little hazardous, as France was at war with the English and Dutch. All VOC ships had therefore to use the Northern route, which accounted for a number of known VOC wrecks on Scotland's and Ireland's coasts.

Peter McBride located the *Santo Christo de Castello,* a Genoese merchantman that was wrecked off Cornwall in 1667. With Richard Larn and Ron David he has retrieved a number of beautifully preserved artifacts. He also located the British man o'war *Coronation* which sank in a storm with the loss of 600 men in 1691. An 87-gun ship-of-the-line, *Coronation* was found in 60 feet of water off Penlee Point, Plymouth.

As with most old wrecks the first signs of the *Coronation* was a cannon. Three intensive diving days later, eleven more cannon and three anchors had been located. Identification was subsequently made through the retrieval of a pewter plate that had stamped upon it the maker's name and a crest confirmed to be that of the Skelton family. Charles Skelton had been captain of the *Coronation* and was a son of the then Lieutenant-Governor of Plymouth.

The wreck of a vessel that sank in 1520 at Cattewater has also been found. The *Mary Rose,* which sank at Spithead in 1545, has been identified. So have the *Grâce Dieu* built by Henry V and burnt in the Hamble River in 1439; the *Amsterdam,* a VOC ship of that Chamber which foundered during a storm in 1749 and was buried in sand at Hastings; the *Mary* wrecked off the Skerries, Anglesey, in 1675; the *Assurance* sunk off the Needles, Isle of Wight, in 1738; HMS *Dartmouth* wrecked in 1690 off the Isle of Mull; and the *Anne* wrecked off Hastings, 1690. None of these vessels contained any intrinsic treasure but all were of historic interest, involved a costly amount of time to survey and merited protection from predatory divers.

The greatest concentration of European wrecks must be in the Western Approaches, where more than four hundred known wrecks litter the sea bed and maybe the bones of twice that number of unknown ships. Wrecks have multiplied from the sixteenth century to the 1970s, and despite the modern marvels of electronic navigation, despite lighthouses and lightships and accurate charts,

Schiller, *wrecked off the Isles of Scilly in 1875*. (F. E. Gibson)

vessels still impale their increasingly vast hulls upon the rocks.

The effects of a number of these wrecks were auctioned in September 1975, for the first time by a local auctioneer, William Lane & Son, in a local town, Penzance. There were nine wrecks in all. The auction included items from the Dutch East Indiamen *Hollandia* and *Princesse Maria* as well as *De Liefde*; from the British men o'war *Association*, *Athénienne* and *Sprightly*; from the German-American liner SS *Schiller*; from the American sailing ship *Thomas W. Lawson*; and from the British slave ship *Duoro*.

It was a unique auction that would enable those interested in wreck souvenirs to purchase coins or artifacts at relatively reasonable prices, for items were to be sold individually. Even coins, tarnished and worn, were sold singly and an historic piece-of-eight, although merely a sliver of a bright coin, could be bought for something like £10, complete with certificates of authentication. The sale was highly successful.

Of the British men o'war, the only one not mentioned so far in this narrative, HMS *Sprightly*, was another Robert Sténuit discovery, this time from off the Hanois Bank, Guernsey. She was a cutter of twelve guns which capsized in 1777. From this wreck Sténuit recovered English gold guineas and half-guineas, pillar dollars, cannon and many other artifacts that were sold in Penzance.

As for the German–America liner *Schiller*, of 3,500 tons gross, she had left New York on April 27, 1875, bound for Plymouth and Hamburg, carrying 254 passengers and a crew of 100. Amongst her cargo was mail and £60,000 in American twenty-dollar gold coins with the distinctive eagle strike. *Schiller* had made good time and, by May 7, was off the Scillies. In that latitude the liner encountered thick fog and heavy seas. Reducing speed to four knots, she crept on towards Scilly with extra lookouts posted; some of the male passengers wagered a bottle of champagne for the first person to spot Bishops Rock light.

They all missed the light and no one heard the fog bell. At about ten o'clock in the evening, *Schiller* drove onto the Retarrier Ledges and was badly holed. Before Captain Thomas had a chance to drag the liner's bows off the rocks, three huge waves battered her and threw the liner broadside onto the Retarriers. Lifeboats were smashed in the seas as *Schiller* heeled over.

In the morning a fleet of small craft came from the islands to rescue such survivors as there were—a pitiful total of forty-three men and women. More than three hundred had perished. Many of the bodies were recovered and buried in mass graves at Old Town, on St Mary's Island, with scenes of great mourning. More than £57,000 of her cargo was reputed to have been salvaged, as well as other valuable items from the ship. In St Mary's stands a row of houses always referred to locally as 'Schiller Row', supposedly built with money from the *Schiller*. Coincidentally, it was in one such house that two modern day Scilly divers lived, Terry Hiron and Jim Heslin, and it was these two who re-located the *Schiller* in about 50–60 feet of water.

There was a large metal coffee pot, among the artifacts re-covered, showing clearly the crest and motto of the German Transatlantic Steam Navigation Company. Today all that is recognizable below the Retarriers are the *Schiller*'s great propellers, winches and engine parts, scattered over a wide area.

The *Duoro* was wrecked on Crebawethan Rocks on January 27, 1843, en route from Liverpool to Oporto; her master was Captain Gowland. The barque's manifest listed a cargo of baled goods, armoury and brass stops. In fact, *Duoro* was on a much more sinister mission, only disclosed because of her wrecking. She was a slave ship, operating illegally. Ten years previous to her sailing, slavery had been abolished throughout the British Empire.

The *Duoro*'s entire crew perished; only six bodies were recovered, floating upon the tide, together with the barque's figurehead. It was only when Hiron and Heslin located the wreck and discovered her cargo that the true, unsavoury mission of the *Duoro* came to light. Some of the cargo was indeed armoury but 'baled goods and brass stops' as listed, turned out instead to be Aggries and Manillas, goods with which to purchase slaves in West Africa for resale in the Southern states of America of the West Indies, to work in the cotton or sugar plantations. A Manilla was a small bronze hoop with open ends; the currency rate was one Manilla for one slave. Aggries were cut-glass blue beads and were more highly prized by the African Chiefs, the rate of exchange being one Aggrie for seven slaves.

Manillas were particularly prized by the Benin tribesmen, who melted down the bronze to fashion their own Benin bronzes. These figures are today greatly esteemed in Western culture. They change hands for many thousands of pounds and the acquisition of Benin bronze is high on many a renowned collector's list. It is strange to consider that Manillas churned out in their thousands in Birmingham would enable the return to the London fine art market of highly sought-after sculpture, having in the meantime purchased a number of slaves for the new Americans!

A number of Aggries and Manillas were on offer from the *Duoro* at the Penzance auction. There were also clay pipe bowls, musket side plates, trigger guards, rammer ferrules and musket flints.

The *Thomas W. Lawson* was the third wreck re-located by Hiron and Heslin in the Scillies from which artifacts were offered for sale at Penzance. Although constructed in this century, in 1902, and made of steel, she was in fact the largest ever pure sailing ship. She was built by the Fore River Engineering Company of Quincy, Massachusetts, to prove that large sailing vessels with a small crew could be more economic than contemporary steam ships. With an overall length of 395 feet (120 metres) and a gross weight of 10,000 tons, she was capable of carrying 7,500 tons of cargo. Power came from twenty-five sails totalling a canvas spread of 40,500 square feet rigged on seven steel masts. Each mast was named after a day in the week. Despite her size the *Lawson* required a crew of only eighteen to work her effectively. At the base of each mast a donkey engine was harnessed to warps which enabled sail to be hoisted or lowered without the crew going aloft.

Deep Sea Treasure

November 20, 1907 saw the *Thomas W. Lawson* outward bound from Philadelphia for London with a cargo of two-and-a-quarter million gallons of paraffin valued at £40,000. Her master, Captain Geoffrey Dow, and her small crew endured a terrible Atlantic crossing beset with gale after gale; so appalling had the crossing been, indeed, that as she approached Scilly only six sails remained in use and all her boats had been swept away. By December 13 the *Lawson* was within the Bishops Rock and among the Westerns. She anchored up, hoping to ride out another freshening north-westerly. Throughout the night the storm intensified, despite which St Agnes' sail-and-oar lifeboat had stood by the *Lawson*, leaving only as winds reached force ten. One Scillonian, William Cook Hicks, the Trinity House Pilot, went aboard the *Lawson* to assist Captain Dow should he require piloting through the treacherous Scillies rocks.

During the hours of early morning the storm caused *Lawson*'s cables to part and, in minutes, the great ship was cast upon Carn Irish and was broken in two. The St Agnes gig *Slippen* put out in tremendous seas and found three survivors including Captain Dow and his engineer, Edward Rose, the two latter being rescued by Freddy Hicks who swam to them through heaving seas with a rope around his waist. Alas, his father, William Hicks, who had stayed with the *Lawson* overnight, lost his life in the wreck. For their great courage every member of the *Slippen*'s crew received a gold medal and Freddy Hicks a gold watch from both the *Lawson*'s owners and the United States Government.

The *Lawson* was re-located by Hiron and Heslin in fifty feet of water. The two halves of the ship lay almost five hundred yards apart. The wreck itself is very broken up but the *Lawson* is recognizable from her tanks and hollow masts which are so huge that a diver, if he cares to, can swim up inside them.

Altogether just over 1,500 coins and artifacts from the nine wrecks were sold at the Penzance auction, for a total of £40,000. Wreck items were certainly becoming a new collector's speciality and those collectors who had to compete with numismatists and historians were quite prepared for prices to rise with inflation: the demand was outstripping the supply.

Successful though similar auctions proved to be, the final share-out of treasure proceeds often led to disputes—or at least mis-understandings—amongst team members. The trouble was that the

By the basket-full. Terry Hiron and Jim Heslin examine a fine gold ring chain found among thousands of silver and gold coins. (F. E. Gibson)

top line of monies received at auctions bore little relation to the bottom line of monies eventually shared out and a number of hot-blooded divers fell out with team-leaders and colleagues over the division of the rewards. You might say that this was true to tradition. Treasure spoils led to friction from the days of pirates to the division of prize money in the 'King's Navee'.

Friction was hardly surprising, because of the complex nature of accounting. An auctioneer required fees for his services, catalogues had to be printed and advertisements placed. H.M. Receiver of Wreck incurred expenses. The Treasury required its percentage. There were transportation charges—no small amount where cannon were involved—postal and telephone charges, hotel expenses, boat hire charges and last but by no means least conservation charges. After the deduction of all these came the deduction of the organizers' expenses, team wages and fees. Even the air that the divers breathed underwater had, of course, to be bought.

Most of the professional divers hired were paid at a daily rate plus an agreed bonus at the end of an auction or an agreed percentage of the net proceeds of a treasure sale. Many could be forgiven for believing totally erroneous newspaper headlines with almost fictitious estimates of the worth of some treasure. They saw a figure printed in black and white in the national newspapers and they wanted to know why they ended up with a few meagre pounds. In the early days controversy over the final share-out culminated in a swap round of teams until the divers settled down into compatible groups and acquired a greater understanding of the problems of certain expenses.

For example, the necessary conservation of artifacts and the cleaning of coins and cannon were a great deal more costly than many realized. If a team were not able to conduct such work themselves the expert attention needed to clean and preserve bronze and silver took a large slice of the gross profit. Luckily for Morris and Sténuit, their own knowledge of conservation work saved their teams thousands of pounds. Both have laboratories capable of treating the largest items.

A cannon sold at auction for £4,000 might incur the following expenses, deductible from that sum:

Auction price	£4,000
Auction fees ten percent of realized price plus catalogue—and special advertizing	500
H.M. Receiver of Wreck expenses	200
Conservation expenses	1,500
Transportation from site to auction	250
Team-leader's hotel and auction expenses	50
	£2,500
First line profit	£1,500
Less: boat hire and team expenses for recovery of cannon	500
Bottom line profit	£1,000

Only then does the share-out begin. Usually, a team-leader would take the major portion, for he put up the original capital and took the financial risks. Possibly he would take one-third, leaving two-thirds to be shared out amongst the team, which might total a minimum of eight members. From a £4,000 cannon, therefore, a diver might end up with something like £84, not a fortune by any means. In the case of a cannon the Treasury waives the right to a percentage. On coins or items of gold or jewellery or any other item of intrinsic value the Treasury, the State, or foreign Government would take between 25% and 33⅓% from the net auction price, reducing the share-out still further.

Of course, vessels such as the *Association*, *Hollandia* and *Girona* produce enough gross rewards to enable each team member to gain substantially. But it has to be a very good wreck discovery to satisfy everybody and it is hardly surprising that the temptation remains for a diver or divers to circumvent colleagues, team-leaders and the Receiver of Wreck. A gold coin can easily be secreted and may be worth anything up to £800, without any deduction for expenses. It is impossible, even imprudent, to say to what extent authorities in Europe, Central and North America and South America are duped out of their required percentage. As with all things recovered from the sea for generations past, there are certain traditions, which may not be condoned yet may be secretly admired, involved in such activities as wrecking, smuggling, piracy, privateering, contraband, bootlegging, freetrading or whatever name may be currently employed.

It was King Richard I who began a tax on imported goods, and from his reign sprang the smuggler—rascal or 'Gentleman of the Trade', depending on the point of view. Successive generations rebelled against duties on a variety of goods. In Boston, Massachusetts, the duty on tea reached an unacceptable high; in England it was the duty on tobacco and brandy that led to revolt. Nowhere did smuggling or 'free-trading' become such an organized industry as in south-west England, particularly Cornwall, for it lay opposite Brittany, had plenty of small boats, expert seamen and ill-paid miners—'tinners', earning only mere survival money to keep their families from starving—men quite willing and eager to 'run' a barrel of brandy from ship to customer for the equivalent in one night of a whole week's wages.

It was not just the poor who benefited from 'free-trading'. The customers for smuggled goods included the gentry, magistrates, clergy, doctors, and even the ladies—for French and Belgian silks. Smuggling luggers were often built and operated from money supplied by a consortium of landowners. 'Free-trading' became an accepted way of life throughout the West Country and hard though successive Governments tried to stamp out such illegal activities, the 'Gentlemen of the Trade' flourished.

There has been a long, often painful, history of fighting between the Excise men and the 'Free-traders' of the West Country. Perhaps it is the fact that most Receivers of Wreck are members of the local Customs and Excise office that rekindles in some divers a resentment that lies half-buried in the past. Be that as it may, there have been occasions in the recent past when certain divers and Customs Officers have not seen eye to eye.

However, it is not only the Western Approaches to the English Channel that have their stories of adventure, and their tales of treasure. All over the world, along one-time sailing ship routes, wrecks are being located. Off South Africa near Port Elizabeth, David Allan and Gerry van Niekerk located the remains of a Portuguese carrack, *Sacramento*, and these two divers have recovered from the wreck forty bronze cannon—a unique achievement, conducted under extreme conditions of heavy surf and fast currents. Hampered both by bad weather and pirate divers— apparently, an international brigade—the two South Africans are to be congratulated on their success. 'Their' cannon range from 'perfect' to 'poor', some being badly scoured by sea bed action. Currently both divers are working on the wrecksite of a British man o'war, HMS *Dodington*. David Allan, with his black moustache and slim build, physically resembles Robert Sténuit but the resemblance does not stop there. Like Sténuit, Allan quietly engages in a vast amount of research.

Another diver with a well-deserved reputation is the American Robert Marx, a truly great diver in every sense of the word. Now in his early forties, Marx first came to prominence when for three years he led an archaeological team excavating the sunken city of Port Royal, part of which disappeared beneath the sea in an earthquake in 1692. Originally trained in the U.S. Marine Corps as a diver, Marx has worked as a consultant marine archaeologist for the governments of Jamaica, Panama, Colombia, Lebanon, Tunisia, Portugal and Spain.

Marx was the organizer and navigator of the *Nina II*, an authentic reproduction of the Columbus original which he sailed from Spain to San Salvador, retracing the famous explorer's voyage. For this and other marine services, Marx was created a Knight Commander of Isabel the Catholic by a grateful Spanish Government.

In twenty years of diving exploration his treasure finds amount to a staggering total value of more than $10,000,000. He is still locating yet more wrecks. One of his marvellous treasure finds has been that of the *Nuestra Senora de la Maravilla* that sank on the Little Bahama Bank during one stormy night in January 1656. The *Maravilla* was reputed to carry five million pesos worth of gold, silver and precious stones. There was also reputed to be on board a solid gold statue of the Virgin and Child.

Marx also knows the value of research. In Seville's archives of the Indies he found many documents in original Castillian script referring to the *Maravilla*. Additionally he found a small journal that had been written by a survivor of the wreck. Armed with copies of these and with three old charts of 1650 which referred to the location of the wrecked galleon, Marx was convinced he could relocate the *Maravilla*. A most important document later came into his hands, that of the cargo manifest, which listed the entire contents at the time of her wreck. Marx knew that an attempt to salvage items had been made by the Spanish in 1656 but further documents declared that only 450,000 pesos worth had been recovered.

Leading a team of divers Marx did locate the *Maravilla*, by spotting ballast stones well known as the type used in such vessels. He began to retrieve a considerable haul of treasure from under many feet of sand. One day's find included an exquisitely scallop-shaped gold dish, silver spoons and snuff boxes, brass navigational dividers and a 72 lb silver ingot complete with stamps of the Ensayador and duty-paid indentations. Another day saw the recovery of six hundred silver coins, a number of silver plates and small silver bars. The coins were stamped with the letters of Potosi, Lima and Mexico City mints. Gold coins were soon found and, at one time, five silver bars weighing about 70 lb each were lifted together. Two thousand silver coins were found at the beginning of another day's dive.

Within a few days the Marx team had recovered over $200,000 worth of gold and silver coin, precious stones and artifacts. Yet they were still only scraping the surface of the wreck. It was time to seek more diving help, but caution and a sense of security were wise. Already five vessels belonging to pirate divers had been chased away. Sharks were a periodic menace, sometimes requiring the use of explosive spears. The team worked at an exhausting rate, for once they left the wreck there was no telling what the modern day pirates would pillage, even though Marx had official Bermudan Government sanction to work the wreck. Within a couple of months Marx estimated he had recovered more than $2,000,000 worth. The whole team was ecstatic—until the political arguments began.

Robert Marx's company—Seafinders Incorporated—had been given permission to store all items retrieved from the wreck in a Florida bank pending a division with the Bermudan Government. But following a re-shuffling of cabinet ministers a new Bermudan ruling insisted that all finds be delivered and kept in Bermuda. The new minister refused to honour the previous minister's agreement. In order to enforce the delivery of treasure to Bermuda the Government revoked Seafinders' license. Under threat of arrest Marx had to suspend operations. After the treasure had been delivered to Bermuda there were further delays in the division of the treasure so far found and in permission for further diving, because other divers claimed that they had discovered the wreck first and that Marx had not handed in everything he himself had found.

The Bermudan Government did not for one moment believe these reports but an investigation had to be carried out. This completely cleared Seafinders and vindicated Marx. The delays are over at last and diving has resumed. Perhaps the gold statue of the Virgin and Child may yet be recovered. Nonetheless, it was an aggravating set-back for Marx who has and always will carry out his excavations in a proper manner and not resort to the massive use of explosives which pirate divers use to clear sand and ballast stones, to seize treasure quickly before Government or State is aware what is happening. Sunken treasure is becoming very big business indeed.

In Florida, in recent years, a treasure seeker by the name of Tom Gurr hit the national newspapers after locating the wreck of a Spanish galleon, *San Jose*, that with other vessels of the 1733 Plata Flota was lost in a hurricane off Plantation Key. Because the wrecksite was outside the three mile limit Gurr believed that he did not require a permit from the Florida Board of Archives and History. When stories of Gurr's finds began to circulate, escalating into fictional 'millions of dollars' worth', the State of Florida arrested him and charged him with salvaging a wreck without permission. Gurr accepted their ruling on ownership, received a salvage permit and went back to work. But the matter did not rest there.

Tom Gurr completed his salvage work on the *San Jose* in the autumn of 1973. In December the Florida Board advised him that their representatives would collect all treasure items from him in January (1974). That was the point at which C.B.S. news cameras showed pictures of Gurr throwing back into the sea items he had previously salvaged. Gurr complained that, since the State of Florida had refused to give him a division of treasure over the past years, he was now bankrupt and was returning everything to where he had found it.

Again he was arrested, charged with grand larceny because the State maintained that he had thrown away State property. State divers were sent to the sea bottom but could not find any trace of the treasure. They searched a canal behind his house and found some missing artifacts of little monetary value. State officials and a number of Gurr's associates then alleged that he had not in fact thrown back into the sea any items of value, allegations that Gurr vigorously denied.

Finally the F.B.I. joined the action after investigations revealed that $30,000 worth of coins were due to be auctioned in Los Angeles on February 6. Tom Gurr claimed that these coins were salvaged before he was forced to obtain a State salvage permit. This claim was disputed by the State. Subsequently, the State confiscated all the coins due to be auctioned and Gurr was dealt with by the Courts. Despite a certain amount of general sympathy for Gurr, it was a salutary lesson for all divers.

Another salutary lesson was learnt by Jack Slack and two other Americans, Gary Simmonds and Dick Tindell, after they came across a Spanish wreck off Bermuda's Freeport. In very shallow water, amid spectacular coral reefs, they discovered a treasure of 10,000 pieces-of-eight, conservatively valued at $3,000,000. All three being fit, healthy and reasonably young men, their natural exuberance at such a find surfaced with glee; their optimism was unfortunately torpedoed by their incredible naivety as businessmen.

Capital was needed to salvage the rest of the wreck's artifacts and specie. Capital was found in return for a percentage of the treasure. The Bermudan Government was also entitled to a percentage. So was the business manager hired to handle the marketing and promotion of all ancillary rights. There was a contract for this . . . a contract for that . . . film, book and photographic rights . . . a percentage here . . . a percentage there. . . . They signed their names on every dotted line and were given even more help than they needed. They were helped out of a fortune. After two exhausting and frustrating years, Jack Slack sold out his share of the treasure for a little more cash than he had before the wreck was discovered. Subsequently, he wrote a book entitled *Finders, Losers* (Harcourt Brace), that sets out the whole sorry business and illustrates graphically that all the sharks are by no means in the sea!

IO

The Tale of Simon Burton's Cannon

The story of Simon Burton's cannon is more heartening than the experiences of either Tom Gurr or Jack Slack. It proves, moreover, that treasure hunting can be done by anyone who keeps his eyes open and is careful. Teignmouth is an old English Channel port in South Devon, situated on Lyme Bay. Its rolling red hills and sandy beaches have been a favourite tourist spot for many years. It is also famous among anglers for its flounders. On a hot summer evening— July 28, 1975—thirteen-year-old Simon was spear-fishing for flounder in fairly shallow water, about 150 yards out from one of Teignmouth's most popular beaches. Simon was wearing a wet-suit but had no air tank, only a facemask and snorkling tube; he held a trident spear in his hand.

He was watching carefully for a flounder's tell-tale eye opening and closing, for that is the only part of the fish that can be seen as it conceals itself beneath a covering of sand. Then, in his words, 'I saw a massive and very green looking piece of pipe. With a closer look, I noticed it had two blobs of metal on the sides. It suddenly came to mind it was a cannon!' He surfaced for a breath and dived down again. He cleaned a little sand from off the top and discovered markings and what looked like a crest. The cannon appeared to be about nine feet long. Lungs almost bursting, he surfaced for another breath before diving yet again to inspect his prize.

The do-it-yourself Burton family ready to transport the sixteenth century Venetian cannon home for cleaning—the result of Simon Burton fishing for dabs and catching instead £7,000 of bronze ordnance. A bored-looking Simon rests a proprietorial hand upon 'his' cannon. (Teignmouth & Dawlish Advertiser)

A French cannon covered in sea growth comes to the surface in English Channel waters. Work on identifying the wreck continues. (Dave Burrell)

Simon comes from a large family of enthusiastic skin-divers. More than most boys of his age, perhaps, he realized the possible significance of his find. Quickly, he contacted his father, Phillip, a retired mechanical engineer, and his elder brother Mark. The three Burtons returned to the spot and investigated underwater. Phillip Burton deduced the metal was bronze and therefore had a scrap value of several hundred pounds. That alone made it worth the effort to retrieve. He guessed its weight would be several tons and enlisted a friend's support, a well-known local Trinity House pilot, Syd Hookes.

The following day, at low tide, with a boat procured by Syd, the Burtons tied ropes around the cannon and as the tide flooded, the gun rose slowly up from its sandy bed. Keeping the cannon close under the keel, Syd Hookes took the boat back into Teignmouth harbour and, with the use of a hired crane-truck, duly delivered the bronze cannon to the Burtons' house, where it was deposited in the garden.

Phillip Burton had no idea of the legal procedure, never having been in possession of a cannon before, but he did have a son-in-law in the Customs and Excise Service. He telephoned him to ask for advice and was told to inform the local Receiver of Wreck at the Customs immediately, before he brought down on himself a host of penalties. Phillip Burton rang the local Customs office the next morning.

'Hello, my name is Burton, could I speak to the Receiver of Wreck, please?'

'Speaking—my name is Green, Jeff Green.'

'Well, Mr Green, my name is Burton and . . .' But that was as far as he got.

'. . . and you live in Teignmouth and yesterday you recovered a seventeenth century cannon between Sprey Point and Jubilee Shelters . . . brought it into the harbour here . . . loaded it on a

The Burton cannon with a mystery crest. The maker's initials are plain to see—S.A. for Sigismund Alberghetti, a good clue towards identification.

Harvey Plant-Hire truck and delivered it to 44 Haldon Avenue, where it is now lying in your garden. Is that what you were going to tell me, Mr Burton?'

'How did you know all that?' gasped Phillip Burton.

'Oh, we don't miss much, you know. I'll send you a form, 'Declaration of Items Recovered from the Sea'. Fill it out and send it back to me. What are you going to do about preserving it against bronze disease?'

And so the matter was concluded with the necessary official documentation.

A personal visit to Jeff Green brought Phillip Burton up to date with all the facts concerning the Historic Wreck Act, conservation of metals, the Runciman Committee and the name of John Durstan, curator of the Brixham Maritime Museum who, on behalf of the Receiver of Wreck, agreed to conserve and treat the cannon. This visit also enlightened Mr Burton on the situation of ownership: although his son Simon had found the cannon and the family had retrieved it, they had only done so on behalf of, in this case, the Department of Trade and Industry, who, as the appropriate Ministry, in turn acted on behalf of the Crown. The Burtons would, however, be entitled to a reward following an auction. In the meantime, the authorities—and the Burtons—were curious to know what sort of cannon was it?

Phillip realized that the waiting period before auction could best be spent in two ways: systematically both to search the area where Simon had located his cannon and try and establish the gun's origin. He wrote to various museums in the United Kingdom, took a great number of photographs and began to gather in a variety of answers. The first clue to follow up—or so it appeared at first—was clearly marked on the cannon's muzzle. In all, the bronze was nine feet long and decorated upon the chase, just before the reinforce, with a coat of arms; below that, towards the mouth, the letters S.A. were set between three rosettes. By the design and construction the cannon was thought to be seventeenth or possibly sixteenth century.

The initials S.A. were quite easy to check, for one of the most famous families in gun-making was that of Alberghetti. Sigismund Alberghetti was the first of that line, whose years spanned 1485 to 1497. A second Sigismund lived from 1539 to 1610 and a third from 1600 to 1684. The Alberghetti were known to have made swivel guns

Gold and silver from the sea. Golden guineas, Portuguese reis and escudos, silver pieces-of-eight, English crowns and shillings, all recovered from British waters after an immersion of 260 years. (Benbow/Morris collection)

Gold receptacle in the form of a book, from wreck of Girona. *When found it contained pellets of wax made, in Rome, from a mixture of the wax of paschal candles and consecrated oil. These 'Agnus Dei' were held to have miraculous powers of protection.* (Ulster Museum) for the Medici and their foundry was within the Royal Arsenal at Venice. There were branches, cousins to the family, who also cast guns and it is known for certain that a Zuanne Alberghetti (1549–1609) cast guns that had been used in the great Spanish Armada of 1588.

This had been substantiated when Sydney Wignall and Colin Martin had been asked by the City of Derry Sub-Aqua Club to help in the survey and identification of a Spanish wreck that Club divers had found in the sandy bay of Kinnagoe, North Donegal. Subsequently they were able to confirm the wreck as that of one of the Armada's largest galleons, *La Trinidad Valencera* of Martin de Bertendona's Levant squadron. During their survey and excavation of this wreck, a six-pound cannon of Venetian make was recovered which plainly showed the initials Z.A., for Zuanne Alberghetti, cast in the identical position as the Burtons' cannon.

The possibility that they, too, had discovered an Armada wreck was a moment of high excitement for the Burtons. Was 'their' cannon a piece used in the battles off Lyme Bay, where the *Zuniga* had been so badly damaged and the *San Salvador* had blown up? Phillip Burton busied himself with research. He wrote to Seville and to Venice, sending photographs that showed the crest and the coat of arms, and asked for information. He hoped to discover which of the Alberghetti had cast the cannon. There was a theory that the three rosettes cast between the initials S.A. might denote Sigismund Alberghetti III but it transpired that all Alberghetti cannons carried the same three roses motif.

In the sea, the Burton boys had more success. Another bronze cannon was located not far from where the first had been found. This, too, was retrieved. Again the enigmatic initials S.A. could clearly be seen. Then a third ordnance was spotted and raised to the surface. This one was a bronze swivel-gun with an iron breech loader, a superb gun embellished all round the muzzle with a scallop-shell motif surmounted by a bearded face. There remains much still to be discovered about the origins of this remarkable 'honour' gun.

The Burtons advised the Runciman Committee of their finds and Margaret Rule, a noted marine archaeologist, was happy to help try and solve the Teignmouth cannon mystery. It was clear that the cannon could be around the date of the great Armada of 1588. It was a possibility, no more, that all three cannon had been jettisoned with others to bring a galleon's hull up in the water after being badly holed around the waterline. History confirms many such instances. There was even a remote chance that somewhere off Teignmouth lay an unrecovered wreck. It was decided to enlist the Runciman Committee's support in order to ask the Secretary of State for Trade and Industry to designate the cannon site as a restricted area under the 1973 Protection of Historic Wrecks Act. This has since been done. No one knows for certain if a Spanish wreck lies off Teignmouth's popular bathing beach. It is highly doubtful—yet interesting artifacts continue to be found by the Burtons and it is possible that there might yet be more surprises in store for Simon and his family.

Perhaps the best surprise so far for the young treasure hunter came when 'his' cannon was put up for auction in November, 1977, together with items from ten wrecks, by the enterprising Penzance auctioneers W. H. Lane, mentioned in the previous chapter. Simon's cannon was expected to sell for about £3,000.

W. H. Lane gathered in their Penzance showrooms relics from ten wrecks: the *Association, Princesse Maria, Hollandia, Thames, Athénienne, Witte Leeuw, Santo Cristo de Castello* and the Rill Cove wreck and Teignmouth site. The sale started promptly at 10 a.m. with a Charles II silver crown in 'fine' condition that fetched £44. Then followed Charles II shillings, James II half-crowns, William III crowns, Philip IV ducatons, Philip V pieces-of-eight and a 1696 six-pence that sold for £52. The first lot numbers concerned the *Association* and comprised 170 lots out of a grand sale total of 909 lots. Prices were very good: a 1677 half-crown in 'fine' condition went for £32. A 1687 half-crown reached £24, the same amount bought a cob but a rare Philip IV cob went for £400. Altogether the *Association* pieces brought in £3,900.

Lot numbers from the Genoese merchantman *Santo Cristo de Castello* came next and provided two of the most interesting and near-perfect finds sold at this auction. The *Santo Cristo de Castello* had been discovered by Peter McBride after remaining on the sea bed for 302 years. There was a bronze statuette, 'Tobacco Boy', depicting a nude Negro boy smoking a long clay pipe and holding rolled leaves of tobacco on his shoulder. This was a traditional trade sign of the seventeenth century, now very rare, a delicate piece remarkable for the length of time that it had survived the Cornish

A portrait cameo found on Girona. *The Caesar represented has not been identified.* (Ulster Museum)

sea bed. It was sold for £1,600. From the same wreck came a miniature bronze cannon, with trunnions and casabel, only ten inches long yet capable of being fired. This sold for £300.

From the *Princesse Maria* a brass buckle was sold for £12, a pair of brass dividers for £80 and two copper and bronze gangway staunchions for £30. From the *Hollandia* came 370 lots including rare coins and hand guns, clay pipes, brooches, buckles and buttons. A fine gold Bible clasp went for £28 and a 'rare' Philip V piece-of-eight, dated 1732 (the famous date in which the first machine milled coins were produced from Mexico City) sold for £800. Other coins in 'good' to 'mint' condition and with 'scarce' dates sold for good prices: £575, £520, £400. Other coins, varying in condition and rarity, were bought for prices varying between £18 and £65—a piece of history within reach of almost any enthusiast's purse. The *Hollandia* and *Princesse Maria* lots brought in £18,000.

Amongst the *Witte Leeuw* items for sale was a sixteenth century Bellarmine jug, which raised £200. Altogether Robert Sténuit's wrecks, the *Witte Leeuw* and *Athénienne*, achieved sales totalling £5,000. With £3,000 raised by the Rill Cove wreck, only the Spanish bronze cannon from Teignmouth remained to be sold.

The Penzance auctioneer in charge of this sale was the ebullient, extrovert Mike Newman, a bulky figure, always sporting a rose in his lapel, and with an ever-ready fund of Cornish dialect stories— a theatrical figure at the rostrum. A good auctioneer, without doubt, he is enthusiastic and knowledgeable in the 'wreck trade'. He called the attention of the crowded gallery to the Spanish cannon: 'Possibly from the *San Salvador*, a wonderful example of the Alberghetti family of gun founders. What am I bid?'

Starting at £1,000, the price quickly escalated in £1,000 bids. English, Dutch and German bids were received: £2,000, £3,000, £4,000, £5,000. At £5,000 the bids slowed to £5,500 and £6,000. At £6,000 two of the Englishmen dropped out, leaving a Dutchman and

'Sea like shifting mercury'. At the end of a dive, fresh fish for supper. (Dave Burrell)

German bidding still. At £6,500 Douglas Barnard, a civil engineer from Billinghurst in Sussex, entered the bidding and at £7,000 he finally succeeded in acquiring the Burton cannon.

'What do you feel about the price of £7,000?' Simon Burton was asked.

'Fantastic—just fantastic', answered the youngster.

'And what will you do with the money?'

'Well, I'd like to buy a boat and more diving equipment.'

'And you'll continue searching for underwater treasure?'

'Of course—we've got two more cannons at home!'

Simon and, indeed, all the Burtons could feel pleased at this record price for a bronze cannon. Of course, Simon did not receive £7,000. After expenses, including transportation, auction, Receiver of Wreck and conservation fees, the final amount was between £4,000 and £5,000—not a bad sum when you consider that Simon would have been delighted that hot July day in 1975 to return home with just a two lb flat-fish.

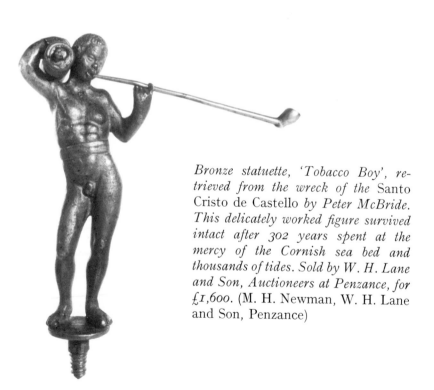

Bronze statuette, 'Tobacco Boy', retrieved from the wreck of the Santo Cristo de Castello *by Peter McBride. This delicately worked figure survived intact after 302 years spent at the mercy of the Cornish sea bed and thousands of tides. Sold by W. H. Lane and Son, Auctioneers at Penzance, for £1,600. (M. H. Newman, W. H. Lane and Son, Penzance)*

11

Treasure for All

A little more than a decade ago most sunken treasure was still to be found in the books of Robert Louis Stevenson and other writers of fiction. The odd coin did turn up here and there, of course, and there was much talk of searching for gold from the *Lusitania*, *Andrea Doria* and other wrecks of fairly recent history. News of the finds of Kip Wagner spread to Europe but their impact was mostly with those who already professed a personal interest in the underwater world. The Florida find was treated as an exceptional event—one that would rarely, perhaps never, be repeated by the archaeologists. Then the discoveries of Sténuit, Morris, Cowan and Marx suddenly made it clear that what was lost to the sea was not gone forever.

Divers flocked to likely areas for wreck location. Because of its tropical splendour and Spanish colonial history, the Caribbean became a skin-diver's paradise, and treasure was certainly a part of the lure for many. Such is the history of those waters, so many tales are still told of Morgan, Teach, Kidd—pirates and privateers—that the lure of hunting for old treasure wrecks grips the imagination of many who have previously only read or watched television programmes. Charted shoals and reefs carry evocative names from the past. Every diver, from the professional treasure seeker to the vacationing enthusiast, dreams of making a fabulous find, a discovery that would, in a moment, make him both rich and famous.

An intact bronze astrolabe, recovered from the Girona wreck.
Astrolabes were used to establish the ship's latitude. (Ulster
Museum)

The sea bed can be a ghostly, weird place at times. What seems to be
a monster stalking this diver is a strange sea growth of coral and
weed. Just don't turn around too quickly! (Dave Burrell)

The tragedy of shipwreck. (Benbow/Morris Collection)

It does happen. There are enough wrecks and plenty of treasure to make rich men out of many. It has been estimated that over a billion dollars' worth of gold, silver, jewellery and porcelain lie on the sea bed around the Florida coast, the West Indies and Central America. When asked for proof of such an astronomic figure, divers list the Spanish losses and itemise three hundred years of shipwreck and piracy. And sooner rather than later, as further evidence, they tell the story of General Juan Esteban Ubilla's treasure fleet.

Nearer home, a number of wrecks have been discovered by members of the British Sub-Aqua Club; quite naturally, no vast treasure has resulted for, in the main, such wrecks are in shallow waters close-in and each had been well salvaged in the past. But such is the number of wrecks around our shores that sooner or later a valuable treasure find will inevitably be made by an amateur diver, the majority of whom have a genuine concern for the under-water environment and a growing interest in marine archaeology.

It has been in Florida that divers have become most deeply involved in the inevitable conflict between treasure hunter and archaeologist, although there are a few signs that this conflict is now evolving into peaceful co-operation. Many divers all over the world are becoming marine archaeologists and a few archaeologists are becoming divers. But when Kip Wagner discovered the treasure off Vero Beach in Florida, in 1964, he unwittingly sparked off a con-troversy that has raged in varying degrees ever since.

Archaeologists claim that Florida's historical heritage is being destroyed by the techniques of treasure-hunting salvage operators: the treasure hunters counterclaim that politicians are using Florida's antiquities laws as an excuse to take over the salvage business for themselves. The politicians say that they are doing their job to protect Florida's archaeological artifacts for future generations. The arguments, like most arguments, contain elements of truth on all sides. Meanwhile the citizens of Florida are mainly concerned that they do not have to dig into their own pockets to pay for new museum halls to display the artifacts or for the con-struction of State departments to administer the archives or for the provision of new 'political' jobs.

One State archaeologist, Carl Clausen, has resigned his post claiming that 80 per cent of potential information is being lost from historical shipwrecks in the blind chase for gold. The official who replaced him, W. A. Cockrell, has been at odds to bring peace into the chaotic situation, in spite of a varied number of personal threats, acts of intimidation and charges that the State is riding roughshod over the rights of citizens and interfering with free enterprise to exploit the resources of the sea.

At the heart of it all, as at the heart of most things, lies money. Florida's treasure industry is no small affair. Many millions of dollars worth of coin, plate and artifact have been recovered from the sea in the past decade. The total number of shipwrecks along the Florida coast is not known for sure but conservative estimates say that it cannot be less than 2,000 and may be more like 4,000. Of

that number, 30 per cent are believed to be of sixteenth, seventeenth or eighteenth century origin: the three hundred-year period of exploration, colonization and exploitation, when vast quantities of treasure were taken out of Central and South America at a vast toll in human life, to satisfy the political schemes and greed of the 'civilized world'.

The situation in Florida is likely to get much worse. The three-mile off-shore limit claimed by the State is disputed by a major oil company. If Florida loses her claim most of the treasure sites now being worked under State contract will become Federal waters. As one diver succinctly put it, that becomes a whole new ball game! Unfortunately, the longer the doubt over who really owns what—State or Federal Government—the more likely is illicit dealing to increase. Divers will attempt to keep their finds secret and take quick cash for their reward, just as they have at times been encouraged to do in the United Kingdom and throughout Northern Europe.

Hundreds of years ago disputes were quickly settled, either by flint-lock pistol or more quietly by cutlass. Now fighting is carried out in a more esoteric manner by use of a court injunction, a High Court writ, or a Supreme Court ruling. The result is still the same, one side is—metaphorically—dead! Such a death can shatter dreams.

There is no doubt, however, that disputes add spice to the story, and danger is an embellishment. The more hazardous the salvage, the greater is the interest of news media and general public. Morris's arguments over the pillaging of the *Association*, Sténuit's confrontation with rival divers over the *Girona*, Cowan's legal battles over *Hollandia* and Marx's political problems with *Maravilla* all heightened their tales. But there is little doubt that each would have preferred a more peaceful plot. For, whatever the advantages of publicity and whatever the individual motivations for their search, each had undertaken an expert and difficult job of work, and one of the most important end-results of that work was that beautiful

A figurehead from the wreck of Young Godolphin, *now in Roland Morris's restaurant, the Admiral Benbow, Penzance.*

and often rare examples of ancient jewellery and pottery were restored for the appreciation of the many who love such works of art.

For those who do not appreciate such art in the form of Greek pottery, many utilitarian items in common day use owe their designs or ideas to the past. For example, carpets and wallpapers abound in designs, part or whole, similar to those found on Sir William Hamilton's pots. His very first collection contained a celebrated vase, the Portland vase, dating from the first century B.C. and from which Josiah Wedgwood, founder of the world famous pottery firm, took inspiration. Wedgwood was a brilliant industrial scientist, who experimented with new raw materials and processes to produce better finished products. It is acknowledged that his finest achievement was his copy of the Jasper Portland vase, perfected in 1790 after many years of trial. We gain more than merely ancient artifacts from an archaeological study of the past.

Luckily, the amalgamation of an old science, such as archaeology, with a new technology—that of self-contained underwater breathing apparatus—can provide a wealth of historic knowledge, and the retrieval of works of art and intrinsic treasure. Many of the ancient and modern wrecks that lie in all the oceans and seas may indeed still be beyond the technical scope of man. But who knows what will happen a decade from now? Already divers breathing mixtures of gases have been down to a depth of 1,000 feet in carefully controlled scientific experiments. As the great space research projects continue, although starved now of the finance they once had, spin-off technology helps many scientific disciplines of which the underwater world is just one.

Of course, the new diving technology is not aimed at the historic treasure seekers, but at the treasures of energy and minerals.

In the course of such mammoth activity, historic treasures will be unlocked for man to study and from which to make gain.

For the present, however, despite the technical expertise that undoubtedly helps many professional divers, the amateur still has his part to play. There is for example, the unlikely tale of a treasure recovered from the bed of the River Thames. A nameless diver recently retrieved a presentation sword equipped with gold handle and guard encrusted with 300 diamonds. The sword is quite possibly that lost by Admiral Nelson, which was presented to him for his victory at Aboukir Bay—the Battle of the Nile.

With wrecks and treasure enough, therefore, for the lucky amateur as well as for the painstaking professional, it is hardly surprising that sunken treasure is a growing business. There is no doubt that whatever marvels, in terms of historical and monetary value, have already been brought to the surface, much more remains to be found.

From the East Coast of the United States, from Canada, Central and Southern America, divers are working on wrecks. In South African waters, throughout Europe, discoveries are being made.

From Scandinavia, three divers reaped a reward after finding $1,500,000 in gold and silver coins from the wreck of a Dutch East Indiaman, the *Akerdam*, which sank near the island of Rundoe, Norway. In Nova Scotia, Alex Storm, with his diving mates Harvey MacLeod and David MacEachern, located the French wreck *Le Chameau*, which sank in 1725, and retrieved 8,800 coins worth $700,000.

From Samana Bay on the Dominican North coast comes the news that an American company, Seaborne Ventures, are on the track of $2,000,000 worth of mercury, coin and artifacts from the wrecks of Spanish galleons *Nuestra Senora de Guadelupe* and *La Tolosa*, that sank in 1724. Clues to the wrecks came as the result of mercury seeping into the bay. By agreement with the Dominican Republic, the company will retain 50 per cent of what they find, with historical and archaeological support being provided by the Casa Reales National Museum in Santo Domingo.

A New Zealand diving team has sailed all the way to the Dutch Friesian Islands with new information regarding HMS *Lutine*, which sank off Texel in the eighteenth century.

And so the romance, the intrigues, the disappointments and, yes, the rewards continue. On November 30, 1979 at Plymouth, Mike Newman for W. H. Lane & Son in their Plymouth galleries, sold 539 lots of coin and artefacts from eight old wrecks, realizing a total of £35,000. A fascinating gold Unite of Charles I (1645) from the Tower Mint, rapidly sold for £800. A William III Guinea of 1699, a Second Bust—Human Harp, in Extra Fine condition went for £550. A 1705 Brazilian 4,000 Reis from Rio de Janeiro sold at £320, a Lion d'Or from Brabant of 1651 for £300. But artefacts also held the collectors' interest in wreck items. From the *Association*, an advanced form of Edmund Gunter's mathematical navigational instrument was sold for £300, and a bronze Calliper musket mould for £120.

From the *Hollandia* wine bottles corked and still containing liquid—one would hesitate to call it wine—surely one of the oldest vintages extant, were found. An ordnance in the form of two cannons from the Church Rocks wreck off Teignmouth, was discovered, young Simon Burton's find. Of these two cannons, one, a bronze minion, probably from Sigismondo Alberghetti's Venice foundry, dated *c.* 1580, has an overall length of nine feet with a bore of $2\frac{3}{4}''$ and a weight of 1,200 lb. A price of £2,250 was quickly realized. The second, a very rare sixteenth-century swivel, has a wrought iron breech and tiller and a bronze barrel. The finely shaped breech is decorated in high relief with delicate shell and cloud motifs. The length is 6′ 4″: the bore, $3\frac{1}{2}''$, and the weight of 600 lb. Bidding for the second, finer cannon began at £1,000, jumped in £250 bids to £3,500, hesitated a moment, continued and finally knocked down at £4,000.

The enthusiast, the historian and the treasure hunter all have ample scope to indulge their curiosity whatever their limitations of time and money. There are a score of *Associations* yet undiscovered, as many *Hollandias*, a hundred *Gironas*—and somewhere a piece of paper provides the vital clue to their whereabouts. It could be in a letter, in a passage in an old record, in Seville, in Amsterdam, in London, or even in a local library. The search itself can be rewarding, the discovery and retrieval thrilling. Examples of endeavour by such experts as Wagner, Morris, Sténuit and Cowan illustrate that application to detail and thorough research are invaluable but experience also shows that it pays just to keep your eyes open wherever you may dive, whether in some exotic island or a mere hundred yards off a popular bathing beach, for the first clue—a corroded cannon or a pile of interesting stones.

Vast fortunes in gold and silver coin, jewellery and plate still lie waiting to be found in wrecks along the old sailing ship routes: golden dubloons, escudos, reis, Louis d'Or, guineas, silver pieces-of-eight, pillar dollars, ducatons, crowns, precious gems, pearls, ingots of gold and silver and an arsenal of giant bronze cannon. The hunt is open, the treasure is waiting—somewhere in the Western Approaches there still lies the undiscovered wreck of a Dutch East Indiaman, with £3,000,000 in gold bullion amongst its remains.

Glossary

Almirante	Second vessel after the flagship.
Almirante-General	Second-in-command of the fleet.
Bell kator	A large bowl or jug for mixing wine with water, as the Greeks were accustomed to do.
Cannon	The overall term for a piece of ordnance.
Capitana	A fleet flagship or the leading vessel of a group.
Capitana-General	Commander-in-chief of the fleet.
Caravel	An early merchant trader of 50–70 tons, fitted with triangular lateen sails to allow close-wind sailing and a square-rigged foremast to drive before a breeze; fitted with up to twelve ordnance for defence. Circa fifteenth and sixteenth centuries.
Carrack	Designed for bulk cargo carrying. A vast beamy ship, a floating warehouse; difficult to handle in bad weather, slow and ungainly. Her beam was half her waterline length and her defensive castles soared high fore and aft. Mostly three-masted with fore and main square-rigged and the mizzen with lateen sail. Circa sixteenth and seventeenth centuries.

Culverin	A French or Spanish cannon about 10 feet long and about three tons in weight, firing a 12 lb ball or shot.
Esmeril	A Spanish cannon similar to the culverin.
Foremast	The forward mast.
Foresail	The major square-rigged sail of the foremast.
Foresail t'gallant	A second square-rigged sail, smaller than and set above the foresail.
Foretopsail	Yet another and still smaller square-rigged sail set on top of the foremast.
Galleon	A compromise between a warship and merchant carrier; with three masts with fore and main square-rigged and with topgallant sails above the mains and also above the mizzen lateen sail. Three or four decks provided cargo space, gun decks and military accommodations. Circa sixteenth, seventeenth and eighteenth centuries.
Galleas	Huge ships, part galleon and part galley, of Venetian origin; three masted but also carrying up to 300 rowers. Heavily armed.
Heeren XVII	'Seventeen men'—the seventeen directors of the VOC.
Kendi	A porcelain pot for tea or warm wine.
Kraak	A particular porcelain glaze finish much admired by the Dutch.
Lateen-mizzen	Large triangular sail set to the mizzenmast.
Maincourse	The major square-rigged sail of the mainmast, above which are the main top-gallant and the main top.
Mainmast	The central and largest mast.
Mizzenmast	The aft mast of a three-masted vessel.
Nau	A vast freighter capable of carrying 1000 tons or more of varied cargo; very broad, almost

round; slow sailing and cumbersome. It was a Portuguese design to cope with their huge East/West trade requirements. These merchant hulks would normally be escorted, although at times they could be heavily armed. Circa seventeenth and eighteenth centuries.

Pataches	A fast, yacht-like vessel often used for replenishing stores or for carrying despatches.
Patax	A small vessel used for storing and transferring wounded men; a general work-horse for the fleet.
Perrier	Smaller than a culverin, firing 6 lb shot.
Pinaza	A fast, cutter-type vessel, used for pilots and often as an admiral's or captain's barge.
Spritsail	A sail set in front of the foremast and to the bowsprit.
Swatow	Shallow cups or bowls for tea or wine.
Tazza	Shallow dish on a stand.
VOC	The Dutch East India Company—Vereenigde Oostindische Compagnie.
Zabra	A Spanish scouting ship, small, light and fast.

Index

Index

Index

Index